DECISION-MAKING CHICAGO-STYLE

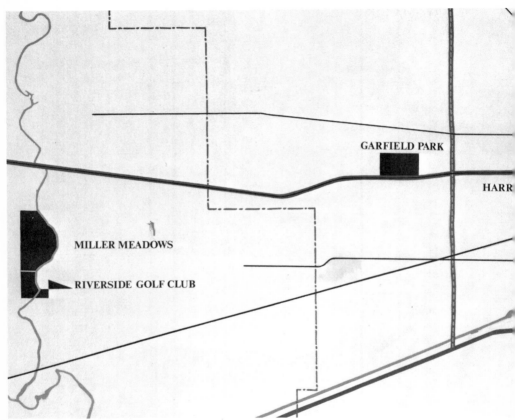

MAP 1 : *Major sites considered for permanent location of Chicago Undergraduate Division*
Source: *Analysis of Sites. . . .* (Chicago: Real Estate Research Corp., 1958), p. 30.

Decision-Making Chicago-style

by George Rosen

U Illinois Press, 1980.

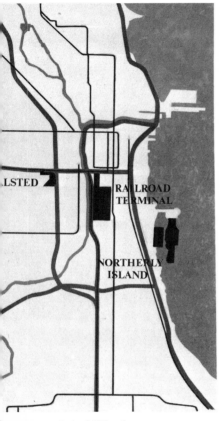

ιe University of Illinois.

Decision-Making Chicago-Style

THE GENESIS OF A
UNIVERSITY OF ILLINOIS CAMPUS

GEORGE ROSEN

University of Illinois Press
URBANA
CHICAGO
LONDON

Publication of this book has been made possible
in part by a grant from the
Stith Estate Fund of the University of Illinois Foundation

LIBRARY OF CONGRESS CATALOGING IN PUBLICATION DATA

Rosen, George, 1920–
  Decision-making Chicago-style.

1. University of Illinois at Chicago Circle — Planning.
2. Chicago — City planning — Case studies. 3. Decision-
making — Case studies. 4. City planning — Illinois —
Case studies. I. Title.
LD2399.5.C5R67   711'.57   79-25643
ISBN 0-252-00803-0

*This book is dedicated to
the memory of two of my teachers,
Theresa Wolfson of Brooklyn College and
Frank D. Graham of Princeton University,
and to the continuing work of
Albert O. Hirschman*

Contents

Maps

Tables

Illustrations

Abbreviations

Author's Papers   Chicago. Personal papers in my possession. This includes photocopies of most of the documents used for this study.

Johnston Papers   Urbana. University of Illinois. Library. Wayne A. Johnston Papers.

Scala Papers   Chicago. Personal papers in the possession of Florence Scala. These include all *Minutes* of the Hull-House Board of Trustees' meetings used for this study.

Trustees' Papers   Urbana. University of Illinois. Board of Trustees' Office.

UICC   University of Illinois, Chicago Circle Campus.

UICC Archives   Chicago. University of Illinois, Circle Campus. Library.

UIUC   University of Illinois, Urbana Campus.

UIUC Archives   Urbana. University of Illinois. Library.

Acknowledgments

IN CHAPTER 1, I give the documentary sources for the material in this book. I would here like to give the names of the people I interviewed, some of whom read my manuscript in its first draft and commented on it. I would like to thank all of those listed. Without their belief that enough material was available to do this study, it would not have been started; without their willingness to be interviewed, their hospitality during the interviews, their suggestions of other people to talk with and other documents to examine, this study could not have been completed. Needless to say, none of those whom I interviewed or who commented on the draft are responsible for the interpretation herein of what happened or for any errors of fact or interpretation. For that I take full responsibility.

I especially wish to thank those who read the approximately 150 pages of the first draft of the section now entitled "What Happened." The detailed comments on both substance and copy I received on that version made possible what I regard the significant improvement of this later version. I have used an asterisk (*) to indicate the names of those readers. The persons with whom I corresponded or talked on the telephone concerning this study rather than interviewed, I have indicated with a dagger (†).

I have broken down the people who assisted me into five groups: (1) University members at the time of the decision (including members of the Board of Trustees); (2) officials of the city of Chicago, either those involved in the decision or those present officials who have been helpful in supplying city records; (3) officials of the state and federal governments in the same groups; (4) residents of the Harrison-Halsted area either at the time the decision was made or later, those associated with area planning at the time or since, investors in the area since 1965, and members of the Hull-House Board of Trustees and staff; and (5) newspaper reporters and private individuals other than those from the neighborhood. At times these categories overlap; in such case I have listed the persons in the category I consider more important for this study (e.g., Earl Neal, a city official at the time of the decision and a member of the University Board of Trustees today, is listed as a city official, since that was the role in which he was involved in the decision. I have listed the staff members of Skidmore, Owings & Merrill as private individuals, although the firm was employed as consultant and architect by the University; and I have listed James Downs as a city official, since his role as adviser to the mayor was probably more important than his role as chairman of the Real Estate Research Corporation or as a Hull-House board member).

1. *Members of the University,* either of the Board of Trustees, administration, or faculty. This group is also broken down to indicate whether they are/were at the Chicago campus (Circle or Navy Pier) or at the Urbana-Champaign campus.

a. Before actually listing the names of those interviewed, I would like to acknowledge the help of former Associate Vice-Chancellor for Urban Affairs Michael Goldstein and Vice-Chancellor for Administration Eugene Eidenberg at the Circle Campus with whom I first broached the possibility of this study and who were sufficiently interested in it to talk with Chancellor Donald Riddle about possible funding by the University to carry it out. On the chancellor's recommendation, President John Corbally made available a financial grant for this study, and Dean Ralph Westfall of the college of business administration consented to the released time that made it possible for me to spend a year working on this study. I would also like to thank Mary Anne Bamberger, university archivist in the Chicago Circle library, and Maynard Brichford, university archivist in the Urbana library, for their interest in this study and their kindness in making available to me the documents under their care; Mrs. Bette J. Boothby, daughter of Wayne Johnston, who allowed me to examine her father's files on this matter, which are now in the archives of the University library at Urbana; and Fred Green, currently director of the physical plant at the Urbana campus, who provided me with the Real Estate Research Corporation reports on the site-location decisions.

b. The former members of the University Board of Trustees whom

I have interviewed for this study or who have read the earlier version are Howard Clement*, Park Livingston, and Frances Beth Watkin.

c. The members of the University administration (past and present) whom I interviewed for this study or who read the earlier version are George Bargh, Joseph Begando, James Costello, Charles Havens*, David Dodds Henry*, Norman Parker*, Earl Porter, Gordon Ray, and William Rice. The help of David Henry and Charles Havens, in the form of my interviews with them and the use of their files and comments, was so valuable that it can only be called essential.

d. Faculty and staff of the Chicago campus of the University, either at Navy Pier or Circle, or both, whom I interviewed, who commented on the earlier version or who ·helped by suggesting sources, are William Adelman*, Andrew Bavas, Shirley Bill, Antonio Camacho, Robert Corley, Leonard Currie*, Lucille Derrick, Sheldon Fordham[†], Rona Frankfort, Elizabeth Gebhard, Michael Gelick, Charles Genther, Leonard E. Goodall[†], William D. Grampp, Mary Ann Johnson, Boyd Keenan, John McDonald, John McNee, Earl Nienhuis, Charles Orlebeke, Joseph Persky, Milton Rakove, Michael Steinberg, Houston Stokes, William Tongue, Fred Trezise, Sylvia Vatuk*, Ralph Westfall*, and Frank O. Williams*. In addition, my research assistant Ahmed Seifi* collected much of the newspaper material and statistical data and commented on the first draft of all the chapters. His help was essential for chapter 7, for which he gathered the statistical material. I also had the benefit of presenting two short papers on my work in the seminar series of the economics department, as well as one before the sociology department; and I gained useful insights from faculty comments in those seminars. Both Geraldine Kennedy and Queen E. Sawyer typed and retyped the several drafts of this manuscript.

e. I interviewed Rubin Cohen, Samuel Gove, and Gilbert Steiner now or formerly of the faculty at the Urbana campus. In addition, Terry Hoffman, a student of urban planning at the Urbana campus, discussed this matter with me in connection with a course paper he was working on and sent me a copy of that paper.

2. *Officials of the city of Chicago,* either former or current, whom I interviewed on this decision or who provided material for the study are Ira J. Bach*, Earl Bush, Gary Calabrese, John Cordwell, Robert

Cusumanno, James Downs, Phil Doyle, John Duba, Tom Foran, Patrick King, Peter LaPorte, D. E. Mackelmann*, Jaro Markewycz (who provided photographs), Alderman Vito Marzullo, Earl Neal*, Mary Rimkus, Alderman Fred Roti, and R. G. Zundell.

My interviews with Ira Bach, Earl Bush, Tom Foran, D. E. Mackelmann, and Phil Doyle were especially informative toward my understanding of the situation from the viewpoint of the mayor and the city; and Messrs. Bach, Mackelmann, and Neal read and commented on the first draft. Mr. Mackelmann suggested the concurrent calendar of Appendix A. Robert Cusumanno's assistance was essential for an understanding of the city's current efforts in the neighborhood.

3. *Officials of the state and federal governments,* either past or present, who were involved in the decision process, whom I interviewed, or who helped by making data available for this study, are Representative H. Woods Bowman, Justice William Clark, Woodrow Kee, Roland V. Libonati, Paul Randolph, former Governor William Stratton, and A. Dean Swartzel. I would especially like to thank Mr. and Mrs. Swartzel for the hospitality shown me during my interview with Mr. Swartzel.

4. *Persons associated with the neighborhood adjoining the campus* with whom I spoke or corresponded: some of whom were involved in planning for the area before it was selected as the campus site or in the struggle against that decision, some of whom were associated with Hull-House, some of whom left the area as a result of that site selection or for other reasons, and some of whom moved into the area or invested in its development after the site-selection decision was made.

Those I interviewed or contacted are Fred Anapol, Russell Ballard, Willie Baker, Frank Bidinger[†], Victor Cacciatore, Oscar D'Angelo, Claire Dedmon, Julie DuLock, Joel Fong and the members of the board of the Westgate Terrace Association, Ernest Giovangelo*, Mr. and Mrs. Sam Godelas, Lucy Guiterrez, Tibor Haring, John Heimbaugh, Olga Jonasson, James Kartheiser, Nikki Malone[†], Frances Molinaro[†], Ron Offen, Richard Parrillo, Mary Pascente, Emil Peluso, Nathan Roskin, Don Sally[†], Florence Scala*, Nelson Smyth[†], and Ralph Tricarico.

It would have been impossible to write chapter 6 without the assistance of Florence Scala, who made available her files concerning neighborhood planning in the area before the University decision, much material—including minutes of the Hull-House Board of Trustees—on the battle she led against the decision to place the University campus in the neighborhood, and the files of her brother, Ernest Giovangelo, who was deeply involved in the Near West Side Planning Board and in subsequent neighborhood planning before the University decision was made. My interviews with them and their comments on the first draft were especially important in my writing of that chapter.

5. Finally, *the newspaper reporters, academicians, and other private individuals* who knew of some aspect of the decision process or its results, who may have tried to influence the decision or wrote about it in some form, and whom I interviewed or communicated with are:

Edward C. Banfield[†], Andrew Boemi, Elizabeth Brenner, Terry N. Clark, Father John Egan, Paul Gapp, Judge James Geroulis, Carl Grafton[†], Donald Haider, D. Gale Johnson[†], James Kokoris, William Korsvik, Fred Kraft, Julian Levi[†], Jack Mabley, Father Daniel Mallette, Ruth Moore[*], Maria Moraites[†], A. Muschenheim[†*], Walter Netsch[*], Donald Ohlson[*], Paul Peterson, Nicholas Philopedes, Mark Rosen, Arthur Rotstein, Jared Schlaes[*], Gerald Suttles, and Robert Werner.

Walter Netsch of Skidmore, Owings & Merrill, the architectural firm that did planning for the campus at many of the proposed sites considered and subsequently did the actual planning and some of the designing at the Harrison-Halsted site, was especially helpful. He and his colleagues Donald Ohlson and A. Muschenheim commented on the draft and provided the plan photographs used in Appendix B. The comments of Ruth Moore and Jared Schlaes on the early draft were particularly helpful in putting this decision in the wider context of the city's plans at that time.

G. R.
Chicago, January 1979

I : *Questions to Be Asked*

In the past economics has largely ignored the processes that rational man uses in reaching his resource allocation decisions. This was possibly an acceptable strategy for explaining rational decision in static, relatively simple problem situations. . . . The strategy does not work, however, when we are seeking to explain the decision maker's behavior in complex dynamic circumstances that involve a great deal of uncertainty and that make severe demands upon his attention. . . .

The study of procedural rationality in circumstances where attention is scarce, where problems are immensely complex, and where crucial information is absent presents a host of challenging and fundamental research problems to anyone who is interested in the rational allocation of scarce resources.

Herbert A. Simon, "Rationality as Process and as Product of Thought," *American Economic Review* 68 (May 1978):14.

CHAPTER 1

Introduction

Our practice [i.e., the practice of economists] is to avoid getting bogged down in actually
finding out about the real nature of decision-making and of the interactions among
economic agents.

> Barbara R. Bergmann, "Economists and the Real World,"
> *Challenge* 21 (March-April 1978):10.

THE DISCIPLINE OF ECONOMICS studies,
among other matters, the decision-making of human beings and
organizations in those aspects of their behavior that call for the
allocation of resources. There is a well-developed theory of such
behavior, and it is a theory that is being extended to a much wider
range of behavior than is traditionally included under the rubric of
economic behavior. In the field of organization decision-making, it
has been used most widely to understand the behavior of profit-
making firms that produce goods and services. Without entering into
a discussion of its powers and limits in that area,[1] one field of
organization activity in which it has been used far less is to understand the decision-making of nonprofit organizations, including city
governments and public universities. This may be, perhaps, because
such decision-making is closely intertwined with issues of politics
and power with which economists have tended to be uncomfortable.

A major purpose of this book is to examine a particular series of
major decisions made by public institutions: the University of Illinois, which is an institution of the State of Illinois; and the city of
Chicago. The decisions that will be studied are those that resulted in
the location of a permanent campus of the University of Illinois first
within the Chicago area and then at a particular site, its present
location southwest of the intersection of Harrison and Halsted streets.
The issue of a new campus in northern Illinois was a major question
for the University of Illinois—the Board of Trustees, the administration, and the various units—over a fifteen-year period from the end of
World War II, when a temporary undergraduate branch was set up at
Navy Pier, until a decision on a permanent site in Chicago was

---

[1] Among very recent books on this, *see* B. Klein, *Dynamic Economics* (Cambridge, Mass.:
Harvard University Press, 1977).

eventually made in 1961. The issue in one form or another was regularly brought before the state legislature and governor over the same period. It was originally brought to the attention of the mayor of Chicago and the city administration in a peripheral manner, but after 1957 it became an important element in the city's urban-renewal effort. It was an issue that raised public interest and emotions to a high pitch. The newspapers devoted much space to it; the local communities in which sites were proposed took strong positions; and the interests of various community groups—business, social, and religious—were involved, and their viewpoints were expressed strongly during the decision process.

Somewhat surprisingly, no study has been made of this entire process, although it was part of the history of the University of Illinois, and the University's records were presumably available. Edward Banfield examined the earlier portion of the process.[2] Various unpublished doctoral and master's theses[3] have examined newspaper coverage of the decision, especially of the final selection of the Harrison-Halsted site, that part of the process which roused the greatest emotion. However, this final decision was only the culmination of a lengthy and complex series of events, decisions, and nondecisions; and the newspapers were only one group among the many parties interested in the decision process.

It seemed to me, because no previous study of the complete decision-making process on this matter had been published, that such a study would be of value both for its historical interest and as a case study in public-policy analysis. Such a study would relate to previous work I did concerning the effect of the decision-making process on economic-development issues in Asia. My membership on the faculty of the University of Illinois at Chicago Circle, the campus that had been created from the decisions under consideration, gave me a particular interest in the decision process both from a historical viewpoint and from the viewpoint of an economist. I came to the

---

[2]Edward C. Banfield, *Political Influence* (New York: Free Press, 1961).

[3]Three theses were especially useful in this study: G. Burd, "The Role of the Press in the University's Search for a Site," 2 vols. (Ph.D. diss., Northwestern University, 1964), thoroughly reviews the entire process; R. E. Anderson, "The Press and the Harrison-Halsted Story" (Master's thesis, University of Illinois at Urbana, 1964); and A. H. Rothstein, "The Circle Campus: The Site Was the Ball Game" (Master's thesis, University of Chicago, 1971).

campus in 1972, long enough after the events had transpired to be able to look at them objectively; and I believed that a sufficient time had elapsed so the participants and those affected could also look at those events and their own actions with greater disinterest than they could have at the time the events were taking place.

The administration of the University itself was interested enough to grant me leave for an entire year to carry out the study. Equally important, I was able to get access to the University archives on this matter, including the minutes and papers of the Board of Trustees; the papers of David Dodds Henry, president of the University during much of the decision-making period; the papers of Charles S. Havens, a major actor for the University administration on the matter, and of Wayne A. Johnston, a member of the University's Board of Trustees over the entire period and chairman of the board's Site Selection Committee.

I also had access to files of the city and federal government with respect to urban-renewal projects on the site, although these did not concern the decision-making process. In addition, Florence Scala, leader of the opposition to location of the campus at its present site, made available to me her personal papers; and the papers of Dorothy Rubel of the Metropolitan Housing Council and of the Joint Action Committee for the Railroad Site were available in the University archives in Chicago, as was a file of related newspaper clippings.

The archives were essential in providing me with details of what happened and with some background. Only in rare cases, however, do files provide background reasons, motivations, and discussions behind the actions taken (and they provide even less material on alternatives not taken). This is especially true of the city papers available to me, but it is somewhat true of all of them. The great value of the papers is the basis they furnished for intelligent questions to be asked of the actors.

Fortunately, many key actors in the process were still alive and were willing to be interviewed. In fact, all of those I did interview were very interested in the study, which brought back to mind events in which they had played a part and which still interested them. It would have been impossible to do this study without their cooperation. The number of persons to whom I am indebted is so great that I have listed those persons interviewed and have thanked them in the acknowledgments section of this book. Unfortunately two of the major actors, Mayor Richard J. Daley and Wayne Johnston, died before I started the study. I was able to interview important figures within the city government around the mayor, who were able to give me some idea of his thinking on the matter. Wayne Johnston's family was kind enough to permit me to use his files, which are quite detailed. I was able to interview various key figures in the University administration at the time, members of the Board of Trustees, and faculty members at the Urbana and the Circle campuses, who had been involved.

In addition, I spoke with members of various external groups that were involved in the decision, among them members of the Harrison-Halsted community, Hull-House, the newspapers, and the state and federal administrations.

The value of the interviews is less for details—memories of events that occurred almost twenty years ago have faded—than for interpretation. Obviously people differ in their interpretation of events, but it is possible to cross-check interpretations and then reach an independent judgment as to the reasonable one. (Where there are different interpretations of the same event I have pointed them out.)

The text of this book was largely completed by July 1, 1978. However, after that date I continued reading on the general issues of government decision-making and came across several additional books—by Graham Allison, David Harvey, Fred Hirsch, and Douglas Yates—that I consider important. While I have not rewritten the text to incorporate their insights, I have referred to them where I consider it appropriate. In addition, two other books, by Lynda Ann Ewen and Devereaux Bowly, Jr., are relevant to specific points in the text, and I have footnoted them at those points.

This is a history of a significant event in the development of both the city of Chicago and the University of Illinois. Both Mayor Daley and former President Henry considered establishment of the Chicago Circle Campus among the major accomplishments of their long and eventful administrations. The decisions associated with that establishment were accompanied by lengthy discussions and, in the selection of the final site especially, strong controversy. The history is interesting in and of itself, and the writing of that history is presented as a straight narrative. Those interested only in the history may wish to skip the more general chapters—the next chapter and the final one—which focus upon approaches to a theory of public decision-making, and should proceed directly to chapter 3, which starts the narrative portion of this book.

This study has a broader purpose than presenting a history of this particular event: it is intended to throw light upon the more general issue of how public-policy decisions are made. There are various approaches toward a theory of public-policy decision-making; some of those will be examined in the next chapter. Those approaches have been illuminated or tested by this case study of how one of Chicago's most effective mayors and one of the University's most important presidents made decisions.

From the illumination this case study provides with respect to those approaches, it may be possible to develop a set of generalizations that can be used to look at how other public-location decisions are made, not only in Chicago, but in other cities and other states by other mayors, governors, and officials of public institutions, possibly even in other countries. One of the most important participants in this process feels that the decision with respect to this campus was unique, so influenced by peculiarly local and changing circumstances that any generalizations based on this would either be so farfetched or so broadly based as to be worthless. He may be correct; but it is important to see whether he is or is not by trying to draw from this experience generalizations that are sufficiently specific to be testable in other decisions, possibly in Chicago, but also in other cities and for other types of location decisions. If this study does do this, it will have made a significant contribution, not only to the histories of Chicago and the University of Illinois, but to the field of public-policy analysis.

CHAPTER 2

Approaches to Public Decision-Making

The core of the problem is that the market provides a full range of choice between alternative piecemeal, discrete marginal adjustments, but no facility for selection between alternative states. . . . By contrast, the political mechanism, through which preference between alternative states could in principle be posed, has not yet developed a satisfactory system for such decisions.

> Fred Hirsch, *Social Limits to Growth* (Cambridge, Mass.: Harvard University Press, 1978), p. 18.

We know very little about the shape and form of . . . externality fields in an urban environment. . . . Changes in them can be a factor in redistribution of income. . . . The political process has a profound influence over the location of external benefits and costs. Indeed, a case can be made for regarding local political activity as the basic mechanism for allocating the spatial externality fields in such a way as to reap indirect income advantages.

> David Harvey, *Social Justice and the City* (Baltimore: Johns Hopkins University Press, 1973), p. 60

IN HIS SMALL but insightful book,[1] Richard Nelson presents three intellectual approaches toward issues of public policy that have been used in making public-policy decisions or analyzing them in recent years. Since I found this classification rewarding, I will use it in this chapter; although I recognize that other approaches exist, one of which will be added here to those he gives, and some others will be briefly mentioned.

The first of the three is the economic approach embodied in such techniques as "cost-benefit" and "systems analyses." The purpose of this approach is to look at several alternative decisions treated as investments, trace through their consequences, and set a value on their returns in relation to their costs so that the one with the highest present value can be identified. This approach derives from the logic of economic analysis, going back almost directly to the Benthamite

---

[1] Richard R. Nelson, *The Moon and the Ghetto* (New York: W. W. Norton, 1977). Another very stimulating analysis and testing of different approaches to decision-making in the field of foreign affairs, which I read after this manuscript was completed, is Graham T. Allison, *Essence of Decision: Explaining the Cuban Missile Crisis* (Boston: Little, Brown, 1971). Douglas Yates, *The Ungovernable City* (Cambridge, Mass.: MIT Press, 1978), also read after the manuscript was completed, deals with urban decision-making and its difficulties and examines various approaches to a better understanding of the process.

pleasure-pain calculus. This is a static technique that compares the anticipated end results of several alternative decisions with an earlier state and with each other. It assumes that a policy-maker can at a given time look at a set of alternatives, trace through the anticipated discounted costs and benefits to the members of society derived from each of those alternatives over time while other things remain constant, and then identify the one that will have the highest social return over the time period. However, there may be no set of simultaneous alternatives facing the decision-maker at the start of the process. If, instead, he is forced to make a yes or no decision on one alternative open at the start that may or may not be followed by a second alternative if the first one is eliminated, the consideration and elimination of any one alternative changes the entire environment and values for the next choice as far as the decision-maker is concerned. In this sequential decision-making, the analysis suitable for the first type of decision-making may not be appropriate.

This method also assumes either a single decision-maker who chooses among alternatives or many decision-makers whose conflicting views with respect to objectives and values are resolved so that all agree. As Nelson points out, "the logic of choice depends on prior specification of objectives, or agreement about the nature of relevant benefits and costs."[2] Without these, differences in interests and goals will yield different results; the process may be less an objective one and more a struggle over the power to make the decision. These problems are quite apart from the difficulties in measuring many of the externalities, whether seen as cost or benefit, that are the theoretical underpinning for the use of government instead of private action. What is the expected value of the benefit of providing city officials and business firms with access to the intellectual resources of a university or the expected value of the loss that may result from the destruction of part of a neighborhood?

The second approach identified by Nelson is in terms of analysis of the organizational structure of government within which the decision is made. This derives from a political background stressing the organizational complexity of public decision-making and the effect of organizational structure upon the decision. Unfortunately this

---

[2]Nelson, *Moon and Ghetto*, p. 23.

approach lacks a theoretical framework that permits the decision-maker to predict the results of various possible alternatives or to select the most desirable outcome from among alternatives. It stresses the political process of decision-making with emphasis upon the various elements within a decision-making organization (or group of organizations), their relationships to each other, and their respective interests, strengths, and weaknesses. Unlike the first approach, the second does not assume a single decision-maker or an agreement on the objectives and values among the various contributors to the decision. It is also a more flexible framework for expressing the influence and desires of external groups interested in the decision. As Nelson points out, economists are unhappy with institutional arrangements that encourage political bargaining and often favor new institutional arrangements so that the market criteria the economist knows can either govern the decision process or at least exert a recognizable effect. But the introduction of such arangements is often impossible within the institutional framework in which a decision has to be made and would not have been relevant when the Chicago campus location was determined. A second disadvantage of this organizational-structure approach is that it may be unique to the particular set of institutions within which a particular decision is made; e.g., the institutional framework of Illinois and Chicago may be sufficiently unique that application of that experience to another institutional or political arena would be inappropriate.

The third intellectual framework is a science-and-technology framework. The users of this approach argue that social problems are scientific in nature, that the application of science to a problem will result in a technically best result that would override both the economic results derived from cost-benefit analyses and the political constraints which may arise from organizational structure. This approach is naturally appealing to scientists and academicians and has a wider public appeal because of the prestige of both of those groups, who appear to be above the conflicts of the marketplace or of partisan politics. "In many ways, many natural scientists' perceptions of how the political economy ought to be run is strikingly reminiscent of the economists' early perception of the role of the policy analyst. . . . So we return to square one and Plato's philosopher king"[3] (now a scientist rather than an economist). As Lowi points out, there

---

[3]Ibid., p. 71.

is no more reason why there should be agreement on the scientists' goals than on the economists' goals.[4]

Nelson's classification system relates primarily to the individual groups within an organization (or to very closely related external groups) that contribute to the decision. He does not discuss, as a separate approach, one that centers on the wider community, with its interest and pressure groups within which the decision-maker operates, and on the interplay between those pressure groups and the decision-maker.[5] We can consider the community-power framework as a fourth alternative approach.

One of the most important and earliest of the community-power theories is an economic-determinist theory that is related to, although it need not be the same as, Marxism. This theory argues essentially that the dominant economic interest-groups within a city determine the decisions of the city leaders. If there is conflict among groups, the dominant groups will win, and their interests will govern the city. This theory was argued by Hunter in the early 1950s. It was criticized by several other scholars, among them Dahl and Banfield (both of whom wrote in 1961). They presented a pluralistic theory of urban decision-making, with numerous groups seeking to influence a result, and argued that this yielded results which were desirable even if not optimal from some disinterested viewpoint. This in turn has been attacked by Lowi in his general criticism of liberal pluralist theory, which he supports by a case study of decision-making with respect to the location of a scientific institution in DuPage County, Illinois. He argues that separation of the interests of different pressure groups from the broader national policy implications of each of their interests results in a pork-barrel, case-by-case type of decision-making that sacrifices the national viewpoint for selfish local interests.[6]

Each of these approaches—the three given by Nelson and also the

[4]Theodore J. Lowi and Benjamin Ginsberg, *Poliscide* (New York: Macmillan, 1976).

[5]This is not entirely correct. Nelson lays stress upon the consumer groups that are affected by the decision and upon the need to protect their interests rather than those of the producers. His discussion of such interest groups is, however, peripheral.

[6]Floyd Hunter, *Community Power Structure* (Chapel Hill: University of North Carolina Press, 1953); Robert A. Dahl, *Who Governs?* (New Haven: Yale University Press, 1961); Edward C. Banfield, *Political Influence* (New York: Free Press, 1961); Lowi and Ginsberg, *Poliscide*. For a general review of this literature, see Terry N. Clark, *Community Power and Policy Outputs* (Beverly Hills: Sage Publications, 1973). Lynda Ann Ewen seeks to apply a Marxist approach to urban decision-making in *Corporate Power and Urban Crisis in Detroit* (Princeton: Princeton University Press, 1978).

community-power approach—will be useful in this study. The University of Illinois decided to construct a campus in Cook County after a careful analysis of the likely future demand for higher education in the state and specifically in Cook County. But the decision arose also from the administration's sense of the changing position of the University in the state's evolving system of higher education and its desire to protect that position. A possible site was first selected on the basis of a careful technical analysis with respect to both what a campus should be and what type of location would best meet the requirements of such a campus at the lowest cost to the potential students regarded as consumers of higher education, to the University, and to the state and city governments regarded as producers of that service. But those decisions were made in the organizational and political systems of Illinois, Cook County, and Chicago, in each of which political authority is legally fragmented. These are also complex communities with strong business and ethnic interest groups that have their own values and goals, which they sought to persuade the decision-makers to adopt in making this decision. As a result of an extended sequence of decisions both proposing and rejecting possible sites, the final result was different from any anticipated or preferred by the actors in the earlier stages of the process. Albert Hirschman has pointed out the difference between the early expectations and plans for World Bank financed development projects in developing countries and the final results. He posited a "hiding hand," a systematic tendency to underestimate benefits, that led in those projects to reasonably favorable, even if unanticipated, outcomes. The process of selecting the Chicago-campus site and the results of that process have some similarities to the development projects examined by Hirschman.[7]

In addition to throwing light on the question of how decisions are made in government, this study may also throw some light on the broader question of whether the large American metropolis is governable. Douglas Yates, in his brilliant book, has answered this in the negative. Part of his argument rests on what he considers the mayor's helplessness in many areas of city life. While Yates presents general

[7]Albert Hirschman, *Development Projects Observed* (Washington, D.C.: Brookings Institution, 1967).

conclusions concerning city government, he bases many of his conclusions on the New York City experience. His remarks on Chicago and Mayor Daley are brief: "A third style is that of the mayor who possesses strong political and/or fiscal resources but who assumes a passive attitude toward urban problem solving. This is the style of the boss. The boss uses his political resources to maintain political control. . . . Richard Daley was a classic example."[8] This study will have something to say on both Yates's broader conclusions and on his picture of the mayor.

Part II, containing chapters 3 to 7, presents a narrative history of the entire decision-making process and a chapter that examines the effects of the site-location decision upon the neighborhood, the city, and the University. Part III, which contains only the final chapter, returns to the general problem of decision-making and explores the relevance of the approaches outlined in this chapter to the actual process of decision-making used in this case. It seeks to determine whether it is possible to reach generalizations about the decision-making process that can be tested in the future by examining other location decisions in Chicago and elsewhere. This would make it possible to better understand how such decisions are being made today and how, if at all, the process might be improved to yield better decisions.

[8]Yates, *Ungovernable City,* p. 147.

II : *What Happened*

For what is most curiously absent . . . is the explicit
account of how Daley did it. It is as if Professor Kennedy
had written the story of a great chieftain without telling
us how he fought and won his battles.

Jeff Greenfield, "Mythic Mayor," a review of
Himself! The Life & Times of Richard J. Daley
by Eugene Kennedy, *New York Times Book
Review*, April 23, 1978, p. 12.

Early Conflicts and Preparation

Will scientists and scientific approaches to decision-making lead us to a better
[decision-making] process? Will the policy outcome of such a process be any better than
that of their predecessors?

Theodore J. Lowi and Benjamin Ginsberg, *Poliscide*
(New York: Macmillan, 1976), p. 30.

THE NARRATIVE PORTION of this study describes the agencies that made the various decisions required for selection of a campus site and traces the history of negotiations among those agencies that resulted in the selection of Chicago Circle campus. To use an economic analogue, this may be compared to a series of negotiations between monopolists, as in such a monopoly situation there is a wide range of indeterminacy in the possible result, depending largely on the strengths of the various bargainers. The University of Illinois may be looked upon as the demander: it had first to decide to build a campus in northern Illinois and then, after that first decision, to select an acceptable site. It did reach a decision to build a campus, and it did select a possible site. Then it had to negotiate with suppliers of the land for the preferred site and for funds to buy the land, that is, with the Forest Preserve District of Cook County and the state government.

The University's first-stage negotiations proved unsuccessful. It then negotiated simultaneously with the city of Chicago, most notably with Mayor Daley, who agreed to contribute funds for a site within the city itself, and with the state government for funds to implement the mayor's decision. The city, meanwhile, sought to identify an acceptable site and to negotiate its purchase with the owners. This, too, failed at first; then the city had to offer land within its own control, although that land had been previously committed to other uses.

While this was going on, the University was successful in its efforts to get funding from the state government. After these steps, the city directly and the University indirectly still had to meet the challenge of those people living in the neighborhood selected for the campus site who objected to the change in land use, many of whom would be displaced by the change. This narrative section contains the story of that process, and it concludes with an examination of the consequences of that selection.

A major actor in the entire process was the University of Illinois. It was the public agency which decided that it wished to locate in Chicago or Cook County and which then looked for an appropriate site. The University was not a monolith, however, and various subgroups helped shape the attitudes of its final decision-makers: the members of its Board of Trustees and its president. From the date the subject of a Chicago campus became urgent until the final decision was reached in 1961, the University had three presidents, and its board underwent at least one major turnover in membership.

In the early stages of decision-making, the main arena of negotiation for the University was the state legislature. The legislature appropriated funds for the University and by its appropriations made the campus possible. In addition, the legislature, by its resolutions and legislative commissions, provided statements of public interest and support. In formulating such statements and making appropriations, it served as an arena for various actors, such as legislators representing Chicago and its environs and those representing downstate areas, and provided a forum for the expression of interest of such other groups as the merchants of Urbana-Champaign, the alumni, other state institutions such as Southern Illinois University, private institutions such as the universities and colleges of Chicago, and community groups. Clearly, too, the Republican governor of the state during most of the decision-making period, William G. Stratton, played a major role. He presented the budget for the University to the legislature, and he urged the bond issue that ultimately made possible financing of the first stage of construction.

In the latter part of the process, once the University had decided that it should have a campus in or near Chicago, the city of Chicago and various other independent and quasi-independent units of the country or city government (such as the Forest Preserve District or the Park District) and any private landowners whose land might be bought or condemned in the process became significant negotiators. But at that stage the main participants were the city and the University, with the University asking for land and the city becoming the major potential supplier of that land. Mayor Richard J. Daley was the person in the city government with major power, inasmuch as his support was necessary for any transfer of land to the University. But the mayor, while the major actor, was himself only *one* actor. Both public agencies and private groups, including the newspapers, were interested in the decision and, by their actions or expressed desires, influenced the mayor's position. As we shall see, neither the mayor nor the University was able to select an apparent first choice of site.

Finally, one of the important elements in the decision process, *after* the city had made its decision but *before* that decision could be implemented, was the community in the Harrision-Halsted area. The factors behind the strength of the community's opposition were the product of a long history of community action. That opposition contributed to a delay in the opening of the campus and had a profound influence upon subsequent public reaction to the decision and the mayor's role in it.[1]

Since many of the institutions and groups involved in the decision were acting simultaneously, either toward the decision or toward goals of their own, I have developed a concurrent calendar of actions showing what was happening at any given time until the decision was reached. This calendar is given in Appendix A. The reader will find this useful in identifying who was doing what at what time and in what order, thus providing a sequence for what must appear to be a confusing series of events.

Before the University could demand the land, it had to make the decision that a campus be set up in Chicago or its surrounding area. In this early period it was the leading actor in the sense that it was the initiator of action. Later on, the city played the initiating role, and the University responded.

The decision of the University to set up a campus can be divided into various stages, with the University at some times responding to external forces and at other times taking the initiative itself. The environment within which University officials made their decisions was never static. It was changing over time and reflective of new pressures, with those changes in the situation in turn leading to modifications of earlier decisions or to entirely new ones. A more

---

[1]For this reaction, see, for example, Mike Royko's *Boss* (New York: New American Library, 1971); and Studs Terkel's *Division Street: America* (New York: Avon Books, 1968).

detailed picture of that shifting environment will be given in the body of this section; but at this point I simply wish to outline, as a guide to the subsequent details, the major stages through which the University's decision-making went.

Although Chicago had no permanent undergraduate campus of the University of Illinois in 1950, there had necessarily been a continued exchange between the University in Champaign-Urbana and the largest city in the state. When the site of the first campus was chosen in 1867, the support of the Chicago legislators was won for Urbana in exchange for the possibility of establishing a polytechnical branch of the University in Chicago.[2] While this branch never materialized, the University did set up a Medical Center in Chicago in the 1890s, and this was the nucleus of what became the largest medical district in the country. The University had always sought to attract students from Cook County, and even before World War II about half the student body came from that area. The extension services of the University had large programs in the Chicago area; the various professional schools in Urbana—law, social work, engineering, architecture, and business—had necessarily close ties with Chicago institutions and firms in which they placed many of their graduates.

World War II and the events following it changed the character of the relationship significantly. During the war itself, the Navy conducted a training program for officers at Navy Pier in Chicago, which was operated by the University. Following the war and responding to the demand by veterans for a college education under the G.I. Bill, the University, acting swiftly in the fall of 1946, set up a temporary campus at Navy Pier primarily to offer the first two years of college to eligible veterans; those who wished could go on elsewhere after that. The intention was that the campus be temporary; but, although it was originally planned for a four-year life, teaching at Navy Pier continued for almost twenty years. A sister two-year campus set up at Galesburg was closed in 1949. Forced to establish a makeshift campus to meet an emergency, the University's initial reactions to later demands to establish a permanent campus were varied. The establishment of a permanent campus in Chicago was considered by the

---

[2]L. D. Tilton and T. E. O'Donnell, *History of the Growth and Development of the Campus of the University of Illinois* (Urbana: University of Illinois Press, 1930), pp. 2–3.

University administration of the period, as well as by very influential groups within the state and the University faculty, as possibly competitive in the legislature with the Urbana campus—a step that would divert necessary funds from the improvement and expansion of the main campus in the short run. In part, this anticipated the end of the G.I. boom and the fall rather than rise of enrollments in the state as a whole in the early fifties; in part, it reflected the continuous poliical conflict between Chicago and downstate.

With President Stoddard's resignation in July 1953, a change occurred in the attitudes of the trustees and the administration. The University was under pressure from groups within Chicago and the state legislature to set up a four-year program at Navy Pier or some other permanent site in the Chicago area. The Board of Trustees, which voted to explore the matter further, and Lloyd Morey, the acting president who replaced Stoddard, set up various committees at the trustee level and at the faculty-administration level to explore the desirability of a new campus and to try to identify a specific location. Since President Morey's administration was of an interim nature and the problem was complex, it was not possible to make a quick decision on such an important issue. But during his administration an effort was made to defuse antagonisms within the University on the matter and to carry out the necessary spadework to moderate or persuade the opposition of the possible need for a Chicago-area campus. Also, the gradual process was begun of persuading private colleges within the Chicago area that the projected growth of student enrollment from the late 1950s on would permit a new public campus in Chicago without harm to them. Perhaps most important, this period of research gave the University time to determine its own best interests in a rapidly changing state scene with respect to education and the University. It also gave the University time to make necessary decisions with respect to the type of campus it wanted and its possible location, so it could go on to the next stage of the process at its own pace once public-policy questions and its own administrative problems had been resolved, leaving it free to act. The reports prepared by the Morey administration in effect provided much of the basic underpinning of data and thought for the subsequent actions taken during the Henry administration.

David Dodds Henry became president of the University in 1955 after a somewhat hectic search process by the Board of Trustees. Henry came with a background of successful administration in urban universities and with an injunction from the Board of Trustees to set up a campus in the Chicago area. He had the benefit of the extensive research of the Morey years and a clear understanding of the importance of the establishment of a Chicago campus.

During the first three years of Henry's administration, the University was the initiator: after lengthy studies of space requirements and programs and a thorough examination of many possible sites in terms of agreed-upon criteria, a decision was made to build a campus at a specific location in the Chicago suburbs. The University sought, through the appropriate agencies in Cook County, Chicago, and the state legislature, to get the desired location and failed. After that failure and a second look at the possible sites that met its criteria, the University recognized that it would have to get a site with the support of, and probably within, the city of Chicago; essentially this meant it would have to work through Mayor Daley. The University's role thus changed from initiator of site action to that of requester of site action from the city. While it suggested sites, urged speedy action to meet a timetable, and bargained with the city to insure that its minimum site specifications, especially with respect to acreage, were met, the initiative was now in the city's hands. The University might suggest, but the city could veto its suggestions. The city's offer was the determining force, and the city's sense of needs and priorities was dominant. That stage culminated in (1) the city's offer, in late 1960, to make the Harrison-Halsted site available to the University in spite of prior commitments to the local community embodied in residential programs for the area's improvement already approved by city and federal governments; (2) the University's acceptance of that offer in early 1961 even though this site had not previously been considered available by the University; (3) the city's override of the Harrison-Halsted community's objection to the location; and (4) the ultimate construction of the Chicago Circle Campus.

This and the next chapter will be devoted to the University's decision-making and its interaction with the state primarily and with the city secondarily. It will be followed by a third chapter on the interaction between the University and the city culminating in the 1960 offer and acceptance. The fourth narrative chapter on this decision-making process will explore the previous efforts of the Harrison-Halsted community to redevelop the area in which the new campus was to be placed, and the reaction of that community to the location decision. The final chapter of this section will attempt to assess the effects of that location decision upon the neighborhood, the University, and the city.

Until now I have used the term *University* as an entity. It will be useful at the start to try to show the University in some greater detail, both in its internal organization as a decision-making unit and in relation to other groups within the state. Within the University the head of the administration is the president. He, working with the Board of Trustees and faculty, sets goals and priorities for the University; his style largely determines how the University will meet those goals; and he is the main agent of the University in its relations with outside groups and the public at large. This is not to denigrate the roles of the trustees and faculty internally or of the state legislature and governor externally. But it is the president who is the fulltime leader of the University, with all the responsibility that implies; and it is he who receives the credit or blame for its accomplishments or failures. Obviously, one of the major tasks of the president, and a necessary condition for his success, is to deal successfully with the Board of Trustees, the faculty, the legislature, and the governor.[3]

The character and style of the three men who served as University president between 1946 and 1965 had a very significant effect upon the decision-making on the location issue. George D. Stoddard, president from 1946 to 1953, has been described to me as a brilliant, forceful executive. As president his first priority was the quality of the University, and he made major contributions toward making the University a top-rated institution. He was also described as impatient and combative, as one who did not suffer fools gladly. His first priority was the Urbana campus and the improvement of its quality; he saw a Chicago campus as a long-run possibility but not as necessary or even desirable in the short run. His relationships with the Pier administration, faculty, and student body were touchy and nerve-wracking. Under his administration, tension built up between him

---

[3]During this period there was no State Board of Higher Education; the University operated as an independent agency.

and the Pier, culminating in public confrontation and open disagreement shortly before his forced and unexpected resignation in July 1953. Lloyd Morey then served as acting president for the next two years. While his position and the complexity of the issue did not make it possible for the University to reach a decision during his short tenure, it was in that period that many of the studies necessary for the future decision on campus location were made, and he brought relations with the Pier community back to a civil basis. Furthermore, at the end of his tenure, he spoke publicly and strongly in favor of a Chicago campus.

Morey was succeeded by David Dodds Henry, under whose leadership the location actions were taken. Henry came to the Urbana campus with a great deal of political strength. The Board of Trustees and various other elements of the University clearly wanted him to stabilize the situation after the conflict and ill will that arose from Stoddard's resignation; he thus came in, at least in part, on his terms.

Henry brought to his presidency an extensive background in university administration in large cities. He had been responsible for developing Wayne in the direction of a state institution in Detroit before he joined New York University in one of its two major administrative posts. He knew George Stoddard and was well aware of the problems of the University. He himself was a strong and ambitious person, determined to lead the University and to continue to raise its prestige and quality and thereby maintain its premier position in the state. Apart from his strength of purpose, he has also been described as good politican and conciliator, able to adapt to the people with whom he dealt and to talk in language they could understand. But he was a tough negotiator, well aware of the position and interests of the University of Illinois. He was determined that his actions would contribute positively to the University and that any immediate sacrifices he had to make would be minimal. The establishment of a Chicago-area campus was one of the major goals of his administration, and he achieved it.[4] In the process he gave up as little

_____

[4]He also sought, in the 1960s, after the Chicago Circle Campus was established, to set up an additional Chicago-area campus and a campus downstate. The State Board of Higher Education prevented both of these efforts. Interview with David Dodds Henry, December 2, 1977, Author's Papers; interview with Boyd Keenan, October 24, 1977, ibid.

of the substance of what he considered important for the University as
was possible.

A number of officers were parties to the University's policy-
making on this matter and had important roles in achieving the final
result. Among these were Charles Havens, director of the physical
plant and chairman of the Physical Plant Planning Committee, who
had the major role in actual selection of the site; Norman Parker, then
head of the department of mechanical engineering at the University,
who played a key role in the development of the academic program
for the new campus and in relating the program to space needs;
Charles Flynn, the director of public relations for the University, who
was a major point of contact with the alumni, newspapers, and groups
in Chicago and elsewhere interested in the decision; Joseph Begando,
who as assistant to the president led the University's efforts for the
1958 and 1960 bond issues; and Herbert Farber, comptroller of the
University and of the Board of Trustees, who as chairman of the
Legislative Relations Committee of the University was the major
liaison officer between the University and members of the state
legislature. Havens's role was most important in the actual physical
selection of the site. In addition, he had wide and discreet contacts
among a variety of Chicago's political and business leaders concerning this matter, so that his insights into local viewpoints and interests
were indispensable to the president and the Board of Trustees.

The Board of Trustees has the ultimate responsibility for governing
the University. It is popularly elected, its members are nominated on
party tickets, and it consists largely of University alumni. During the
period described, it was a strong board: it had forced one president
out and in the interim period had necessarily taken a more active
interest than usual. The board had to approve all actions on location
of the campus, and it had its own position as to a preferred type of
campus. In the early years it saw a permanent campus in the Chicago
area as a secondary need and as a possible threat to the main campus;
but by 1955 it accepted the desirability of such a campus, initially for
a two-year program but expandable to four years in response to
mounting pressure from student enrollment.

Among most members of the board, the desirable campus was as
much like that at Urbana as possible—i.e., a green campus with lots

of land. However as early as 1952, one member, Park Livingston, spoke publicly of the inevitability and desirability of a Chicago campus, possibly in a "blighted area." Interestingly enough, he made these remarks at a luncheon attended by Eri Hulbert, then executive director of the Near West Side Planning Board, who was speaking to inform participants of the work of that board in an area of the city which included Harrison-Halsted.[5] The most important member of the board during the life of this issue was Wayne Johnston, an alumnus deeply committed to the University and, as president of the Illinois Central Railroad, a leader in Chicago's business establishment. Johnston, who was on a first-name basis with Mayor Daley, played a significant intermediary role between the University and the city and between the University and the business community on this issue, while serving as chairman of the subcommittee of the Board of Trustees that dealt with it. Both Livingston and Johnston also were important members of the state's Republican party. Livingston was defeated for re-election to the board in 1958, when a Democratic majority was elected; Johnston was a board member through the entire decision-making process.

While the change from a Republican to a Democratic majority in 1958 had no obvious effect upon the board's policy (the board has never decided issues on party lines), nevertheless the shift confirmed a move toward the city rather than suburban location made possible by Mayor Daley's offer of funds before the new board actually took office in early 1959. However, the final decision on the site rested with the board, as also did the type of program to be carried on at a new campus, since the board had to accept the one and approve the other. It was not about to surrender its authority to any other body, including the legislature, and it vigorously opposed any effort of the legislature to prescribe a site or a program that might limit its power or options. After 1955 all members of the board agreed on the desirability of a permanent campus in the Chicago area, and their support of President Henry on this issue, both within the board and within their different constituencies, was essential to the eventual site decision. They disagreed on specific matters, since they were force-

[5]*Chicago Tribune,* January 22, 1952, for Park Livingston's remarks. For Eri Hulbert's remarks at the same meeting, I am indebted to Florence Scala, who was in attendance. Florence Scala remarks on the first draft of this manuscript, Author's Papers.

ful individuals with their own points of view; but once an internal consensus was reached, they supported what was agreed upon.

In addition, various units within the University had opinions concerning a Chicago campus and sought to bring pressure to bear on the decision in different ways. Initially some of the colleges and departments at the Urbana campus sought to limit the programs at the new campus on the grounds that the proposed programs would duplicate those ongoing in Urbana, and some were said to have argued also that the Pier faculty lacked the quality to do a good job. Some of this opposition may have been warranted at the time, but some unquestionably reflected a fear of future competition for well-qualified students and funds.

The Navy Pier faculty, students, and parents lobbied strongly for a permanent Chicago campus, which would offer at least a four-year program. This arose from a natural desire of the faculty to teach upper-level students as well as a fear of the loss of jobs, the latter especially during the interval between the veterans' boom and the "war-baby" generation of students. Among students and their parents, the motivation was mainly the financial savings to be gained from living at home and working in the city while completing an education. The Pier administration, headed by Dean Charles C. Caveny, strongly supported the campaign for a Chicago-area campus, but its support was limited by its subordinate relation to the president and senior officials of the University.

Those were the major internal groups that determined or influenced the University's policy on the issue of a Chicago campus. There was a good deal of external interest as well. The subject had been a matter of political controversy between Chicago and the rest of the state since 1867. Opposition outside Chicago to the establishment of a large undergraduate branch of the University in the Chicago area was still strong in the 1950s. This was especially so in the Champaign-Urbana area, where the inhabitants felt that a Chicago campus would directly threaten their economic livelihood.

The legislators from that district were highly influential in the state legislature and in the Republican party. One of these, Senator Everett Peters, chairman of the very powerful Illinois Budgetary Commission, saw himself as the protector of the University of Illinois as well as of his constituents. In the early 1950s, Senator Peters repeatedly expressed public opposition to a Chicago campus both on grounds of expense and because he did not "want to see the Champaign-Urbana community return to the great prairie that it once was."[6] He and his colleagues from the area had to be won over before a Chicago campus could be set up.

An additional external group whose members were numerous and influential in the state was the Alumni Association of the University. Some of its members feared a Chicago-area campus would compete with the original campus from which they had received their degrees and that the character of the student body would be adversely affected. The support of the association would also be an important factor.

Within Chicago itself, support for a University of Illinois campus was by no means unanimous. Private colleges, especially those with a local student body, felt they would be threatened by a large public institution. The presidents of both DePaul and Loyola Universities strongly opposed a public Chicago campus and received some support from the president of Roosevelt. All private universities strongly favored a state scholarship program for Illinois students in private colleges as a measure either simultaneous with or alternative to the establishment of a public campus. The opposition of DePaul and Loyola was especially significant, because as Catholic schools they had strong ties with both the Catholic hierarchy and leading political figures in the city, especially in the Democratic party, many of whom were their graduates.

In addition, the University of Illinois's own premier position within the state university system was under attack. Following the war, various smaller state teachers' colleges in different sections of the state had been upgraded to enlarged college and university status with separate or regrouped governing boards.[7] Southern Illinois University was the most vocal of these and had the strongest political support; but, in addition, other universities were demanding funds to upgrade existing programs or to add programs that the University of Illinois already had. Both the struggle for funds for higher education

[6]See *Chicago Tribune*, January 22, 1952; *Champaign-Urbana News Gazette*, April 28, 1954.

[7]This is a very short summary sentence describing the complicated result of a complex process.

as a whole, as opposed to such other purposes as, for example, roads and welfare, and the conflict among the universities in determining the share of each in the higher education budget were important issues in the state legislature. Support of a university within an area was considered a vehicle for possible further power by ambitious state politicians, and geographic lines of division often overrode party lines. At least one of the new universities, Northern Illinois University of DeKalb, indicated an interest in expanding into the Chicago area.

While Chicago newspapers, business groups, labor unions, ethnic groups, and others supported the establishment of a permanent four-year campus in Chicago, that support might have boomeranged if the University did not act. City education officials were interested in establishing a Chicago public university, and other institutions might also see an opportunity. If the University of Illinois did not take advantage of its lead in Chicago by way of the Navy Pier facility, it might lose all and face further threats to its primacy from within the most densely populated area in the state. The period from 1950 to 1965 was one of rapid growth in higher education within the state. While the state legislature was willing to make more funds available than ever before for growth of the state universities, the funds allotted never reached the amounts requested, and growth needs spurred rivalry for the smaller budgeted amounts.[8] It was important for the University to consider the effects of a Chicago campus upon its leading position in the state, both immediately and, far more importantly, in the future. At the same time, conflicting interests and widespread opposition among potent groups to a Chicago-area campus made it essential to move carefully. A false step could create new, or strengthen existing, opposition; the University administration had to use its persuasive power to the utmost to allay or convert opposition. This chapter describes the preparatory stage of that process in detail.

The first stage under George Stoddard's administration was positive in one major sense: a temporary Chicago campus was set up at Navy Pier. The existence of this temporary campus established a base

[8] I am informed that the University of Illinois never opposed another university's request for funds while President Henry was in office. Interview with David Dodds Henry, December 2, 1977, Author's Papers.

that heightened the demand for a permanent campus. In addition, with such a campus even on a temporary basis, it would have been psychologically and politically difficult for the University to pull out of Chicago (leaving only the Medical Center remaining). This foothold also gave the University first choice of refusal in deciding whether or not to place a campus in Chicago—a political advantage for the future.

The pressures for a permanent campus came from several sources. At times the city demanded that the University turn over part of the Pier for other uses. Each time the University had to resist such a demand or the lease came up for renewal, the University was reminded of the temporary character of the campus. On one of these occasions the administration was urged to build up "a strong sentiment in favor of the type of student now attending the Undergraduate Division [or risk losing] our facilities in Chicago."[9] Building such support would also build support for a permanent facility. In addition to the city's demands for Pier space were the well-publicized physical deficiencies of the Pier facilities, such as water pouring through the roof during a heavy rainstorm. Both of these factors pushed the University toward an improved facility of its own on a more permanent basis. But while President Stoddard saw the need for such a campus in the long run and in fact suggested a location near the Medical Center north of the Congress Expressway as logical, he did not give this the priority or urgency some other groups gave to the matter.

Pressures were also exerted upon the University from outside sources. From 1945 on, a series of bills and resolutions were introduced into the state legislature to permit or to instruct the University to establish a branch campus in Chicago. One of the first of these was introduced in 1945 by a then comparatively obscure senator named Richard J. Daley. After Daley left the senate, Paul Randolph, Republican representative from the Navy Pier district, proposed legislation dealing with this matter at every session thereafter. Although these bills were defeated or, when passed as in 1951, were emasculated by lack of funds, they did establish a principle of the desirability of a

[9]Provost Griffith to President Stoddard, February 25, 1952, quoting Wayne Johnston. UIUC Archives, George D. Stoddard Papers, Box 58.

campus. This put pressure upon the University to respond and to at least indicate a willingness to consider the issue even though it was not then in a position to support the specific bills Randolph introduced.

Representative Randolph had the active support from the Navy Pier administration, faculty, student body, and parents for the bills he introduced for a four-year program in the Chicago area. Flyers were printed, demonstrations were held, stories were released to newspapers, support was marshaled from influential groups such as labor unions and local ethnic communities. All urged the need for a four-year campus in Chicago to permit students, who could not otherwise afford it, to go to college. These demands led to an embarrassing public confrontation on May 22, 1953, between Pier faculty and students and President Stoddard.[10]

The subsequent presentation of these demands to the Board of Trustees led to the establishment of a special committee of the board charged to report on the matter. This committee rejected the demand to go to a four-year program at the Pier immediately on the grounds that it should be done in a new, permanent campus which could not then be started; but the committee did recommend that the University begin to examine the need for and desirability of establishing such a campus in the future. The report of this committee, issued on July 25, 1953, was overshadowed by the Board of Trustees' unexpected vote of no confidence in President Stoddard and Provost Griffith on the night of July 24, the subsequent resignations of those two officers, and the appointment of Lloyd Morey as acting president of the University. Aside from the traumatic consequences of these events for the University as a whole, they brought to an end the strong confrontation between the president and the Pier over a Chicago campus.

One of the charges against President Stoddard was his inability to deal peacefully with the Pier faculty and students. While this may have been a contributing rationalization for the board's action, the fact that it was made put his successor on notice that his relationship

---

[10]It was at this meeting that President Stoddard made the remark, as remembered by Navy Pier faculty members of the time: "I made you by the stroke of a pen, and I can unmake you by the stroke of a pen." Interview with John McNee, October 4, 1977, Author's Papers. For meeting with students, see UIUC Archives, George D. Stoddard Papers, Box 59.

with the Pier was important. In addition, the board's special committee to deal with the issue of setting up a Chicago campus was to remain a continuing committee under Wayne Johnston's chairmanship until the issue was settled, even though it was later absorbed into a permanent committee. A permanent forum where the issue could be aired was thus set up within the board. The committee served as the focus of board thinking and made recommendations on the matter to the entire board continuously.

At about the same time these internal events were taking place, the legislature passed a bill sponsored by Paul Randolph setting up a legislative commission to work with the University on the issue of a Chicago-area four-year campus and to report back to the legislature. Representative Randolph was appointed chairman of that commission. Professor Peter Klassen of the sociology department at the Pier was employed as consultant by the commission to make a projection of demographic trends in Chicago and the state as a basis for forecasting future enrollment trends in colleges in the state. This demographic projection was a major part of the final report of the committee and a basis for its recommendation.

In response to the recommendation from the board for detailed information on the need for a Chicago campus and the establishment of the Randolph commission by the legislature, President Morey established a University Committee on the Future Development of the Chicago Undergraduate Division. This was headed by Associate Provost C. M. Louttit and included Charles Havens and Norman Parker as University members and two representatives from Navy Pier. This committee was to report to the president on two major issues: (1) the need for a four-year undergraduate campus of the University in the Chicago area; and (2), if there was such a need, to identify possible locations for follow-up detailed examination.

The committee used University sources to project a 75 percent increase in college-age population in Illinois between 1953 and 1971 and an almost 100 percent increase in enrollment in all higher educational institutions in the state over the same period and in the University of Illinois in particular. The committee recommended that the governor appoint a commission to deal with what the state should do to meet this total increase in demand (which Representative Randolph criticized as beyond its function). It also argued that the facts that over half the state population lived in Cook County and that about half the student body in the University of Illinois came from Cook County made a strong case for the establishment of a permanent four-year campus of the University of Illinois in Cook County. It went on to point out that the great increase in expected college enrollments in the state and in Chicago would permit the establishment of such a public university in Chicago without adverse consequences for the six major private colleges in Chicago. The report did not, however, accept the argument that a Chicago campus was needed because potential students from Chicago with low family incomes would be unable to attend the University at Urbana. Finally, while still uncommitted to a Chicago-area campus, both the interim report of March 31, 1954, and the final report of July 26, 1954, were sufficiently positive about the need for a Chicago-area campus to lead the committee to suggest five potential sites for possible construction of a permanent campus and to recommend further study to select a single preferable site.

On the basis of the interim report, the Board of Trustees hired the Real Estate Research Corporation, headed by James C. Downs, to submit a preliminary report to the Louttit committee and itself that would present a set of appropriate criteria for the choice of a specific site among three classes of sites—high, medium, and low density—and then to apply those criteria in a preliminary fashion to various sites that might be suitable, estimating the time for construction of a campus and the cost of land and construction at each site. Upon accepting the final report of the Louttit committee, which used the preliminary criteria and site reports of the Real Estate Research Corporation in making its site suggestions, the Board of Trustees rehired the Real Estate Research Corporation in July 1954 to make another report. It asked the corporation to catalog all sites of *a low and medium density only* that might meet the accepted criteria, to examine the feasibility of location of a campus at the examined sites considering the relation of a campus to the local government's planning criteria and plans, and to recommend on that basis *the* most desirable site and prepare preliminary plans for the campus at that site. These studies were important, not only for providing the basis for the University's choice of a preferred site but also for associating with the University's location decision James Downs, an alumnus of the University and an adviser on urban planning to both Mayor Kennelly and Mayor Daley.

When the Louttit committee finished its work, another internal University committee with the same name but headed by Dean Caveny of the Pier was set up to continue the in-house location research and to receive the next reports from the Real Estate Research Corporation. One of the Caveny committee's major contributions was the December 17, 1954, report of its subcomittee on physical planning on low-, medium-, and high-rise buildings. This subcommittee reported that it favored a low-rise building pattern (with exceptions only where functionally required) on grounds of educational desirability for the students, as well as lower construction and maintenance costs. It did not consider savings in land-acquisition costs significant, since it argued that the amount of land needed for buildings would be only a small proportion of the total area required for the campus. Most of the space required would be for parking, recreation, athletics, and service facilities.[11]

Simultaneous with the preparation of this report, the Real Estate Research Corporation was carrying out its study of specific location sites, which resulted in what was hoped would be a final report dated February 28, 1955. In its earlier reports it had presented certain criteria for site location that it adopted in identifying a preferred site: convenience of commuting by public transportation or personal car for most of the potential students; a time schedule for land acquisition that would permit the building of the proposed campus to start in 1959 and to be completed by September 1963; a cost that would not exceed $5.00 per square foot; a minimum space of 140 acres, of which about 60 acres would be used mainly for low-rise buildings and 80 acres for physical education and parking; the availability of more space for expansion and new programs if required. The Chicago Plan Commission urged that the choice of site should assist, rather than inhibit,

---

[11]See Subcommittee on Physical Planning, "Report on Low, Medium, and High Rise Buildings," December 17, 1954, typewritten, prepared for Dean C. C. Caveny, chairman, Committee on Future Development, Chicago Undergraduate Division. This in effect argues that the space required should not vary and should not be influenced by cost of acquisition (an argument questionable to an economist). UICC Archives, Box 3, "Expansion—Future Development."

existing community programs for municipal improvement and that any site selected should not have a negative effect on the city's economic and tax base.

The report listed 69 sites as possibilities, including two slum clearance sites which were examined in depth, one west of the Medical Center and one near the Illinois Institute of Technology. (A site located on the map at what appears to be the Harrison-Halsted site was included in this list but was not examined further.) The slum-clearance sites were ruled out for consideration as preferred sites for a combination of reasons: they were crossed by major streets; the city would incur major relocation obligations it could meet only with difficulty; and there was a possibility of strong opposition to a clearance-relocation site within the city.

Within the city other sites were also examined in depth, including several lakefront sites (of which the Pier was one), Riverview Park, and Garfield Park. All except a proposed island to be constructed off the lakeshore north and west of the Adler Planetarium had disadvantages in terms of the criteria that ruled them out as preferred locations. Various sites in the western suburbs were also considered as possibilities in terms of some of the criteria. One of these—Riverside Woods or Miller Meadows as it was subsequently known—was selected as the first alternative site to the lake island.

This report was reviewed by the Committee on Future Development almost immediately upon its receipt. On the basis of comparative acquisition and building costs—$22 million to construct an island of 150 acres on the lakefront, $4 million to buy 300 acres at Miller Meadows, and the higher construction costs on the lake—as well as on grounds of apparent availability, better access to faculty housing and greater distance from other colleges, and transportation problems with respect to access to the lakefront, the committee reversed the Real Estate Research Corporation's preferences.

The Real Estate Research Corporation, in rating Miller Meadows so highly, anticipated opposition on the part of the Forest Preserve District to giving up this land to the University. The district had always been hostile to such requests and had refused to give any data to Real Estate Research Corporation. However, the report did "not consider this an insurmountable obstacle, or a disadvantage which should terminate further consideration of the site."[12] The land at that time served no important recreational function for the Forest Preserve District; the General Assembly might by law require the district to transfer the land to the University; and the district might consider buying substitute acreage with the money it received from the University. The advantages were so great that they far outweighed the potential problem of the district's apparent unwillingness to sell the land, which might change or be circumvented.

On the basis of this report, members of the Board of Trustees took some preliminary soundings on the matter. A decision was not of the highest priority, since it was subordinate to the search for a new president, who would have to agree on the chosen site. Furthermore, funds for the site would have to wait for the 1957–59 budget biennium. In May 1955 Wayne Johnston discussed the possibility of the Miller Meadows site with Edward Eagle Brown, president of the First National Bank and chairman of the advisory committee of the Forest Preserve District. Brown informed Johnston that he would oppose by every possible means the transfer of the Miller Meadows site to the University. Johnston, however, felt this opposition was to be expected and that "we should not be too much upset."[13] Johnston also discussed this with Vernon Nickell, state superintendent of public instruction, who told him that Governor Stratton would not agree to a site either on the lakefront or in the congested areas of the city because of traffic and cost and that he probably would favor Miller Meadows. In June 1955 Johnston alerted the newly elected mayor, Richard J. Daley, to the possibility of the Miller Meadows site; and he commented that, while Daley was cooperative, he was also noncommittal. Thus, although the risk of Forest Preserve District opposition was known, the site was considered so much the best that it was at that time preferred by influential groups within the University.

While this study was going on, President Morey was carrying on discussions with the presidents of the private universities in Chicago. These discussions were at two levels, one general and the other

[12]Real Estate Research Corporation, "Report and Recommendations on Selection of a Chicago Campus Site for the University of Illinois," February 28, 1955, p. 51. Director's Office, Physical Plant, UIUC.

[13]Wayne Johnston to Board of Trustees, Special Committee on Chicago Campus Site Location, May 10, 1955. Johnston Papers, 119/43, vol. 1.

specific, with respect to possible joint use of private campuses in Chicago by the University of Illinois. From late 1953 to mid-1955 President Morey met with various officials jointly or individually. The meetings were held so the University of Illinois might get an understanding of the plans of the private colleges and so the University could better make its own plans. They were also to reassure the private schools that the University's plans were not immediate and that, by the time a campus was established, if in fact it was established, the growing enrollment would fill the spaces available and planned for both the private institutions and the new public campus in Chicago. As late as June 1955, Morey was writing to President Sparling of Roosevelt University that the interest of the University of Illinois was "to obtain our own site and permanent facilities for *our two-year division* which is housed in part of Navy Pier. Even if the University acquired a new site [shortly] it would be years before it would be able to move its present two-year program into the new location."[14]

The private colleges in Chicago were in general opposed to a public campus in the area, and their interest at the time was for the establishment of an Illinois state scholarship program that would finance a substantial part of the education costs for Illinois students at private colleges. As noted earlier, the University of Illinois had urged Governor Stratton to set up an Illinois Higher Education Commission to make general recomendations for dealing with the greatly enlarged number of students in the state, including the possibility of such a scholarship program. This commission, headed by Lenox Lohr, served as a forum in which the private colleges might express their interests; and its report, issued in 1956, was receptive to their needs in recommending, among other items, such a scholarship program.

But, at the same time the University was seeking to defuse the general opposition of private schools, discussions were being held with various officials of the Illinois Institute of Technology (IIT) on the possibility of some coordination or consolidation between IIT and the proposed permanent Chicago campus of the University of Illinois. In effect, it was proposed that either IIT handle the University's

[14]President Morey to President Sparling, June 15, 1955. Emphasis added. UICC Archives, series 3/1/1, Box 6.

engineering program in Chicago or the University build its permanent campus near IIT, including space for engineering students who were to be taught at IIT. This would permit an immediate start on construction of a new campus in Chicago. However, in light of the Real Estate Research Corporation's report against a slum-clearance site and the Caveny committee's opposition to the high-rise buildings such a site would require, as well as the financial and administrative costs such a cooperative plan would entail, President Morey recommended against it to the Board of Trustees.[15]

Apart from the relatively formal discussions with IIT, there may have been some informal discussions even earlier with the University of Chicago concerning the possible use of all or part of its campus by the University of Illinois for its Chicago Undergraduate Division in the event the University of Chicago should leave its Hyde Park location. Nothing came of those discussions.[16]

Another constituency whose opinion had to be felt out was the Alumni Association of the University. The association had set up a committee under Chester Davis to examine the issue of a Chicago-area campus. In early 1955 this committee reported in favor of a suburban campus; but it did not express an opinion on a specific site other than to leave that selection to the Board of Trustees.[17]

Meanwhile, on the important legislative front other action was proceeding. The Randolph commission issued its report in February 1955 recommending the establishment of a four-year Chicago-area campus. Two bills were introduced into the General Assembly appropriating money for such a campus: one by Randolph for $4 million for a site without any specific space limit and the other by Senator Pollack for $5 million for a specific city site—Riverview Park. Both were opposed by the University, which had not asked for

[15]Lloyd Morey to Messrs. Megran, Johnston, and Livingston (of the Board of Trustees), April 19, 1955, with the report of the Committee on Future Development. UICC Archives, Lloyd Morey Papers, series 2/11/1.

[16]Such discussions were mentioned to me in interviews by several individuals who might have been expected to know of them. There seems to be no record of such discussions in the files of either of the two universities. Also, if these discussions did occur, it must have been before 1952, when the University of Chicago made the decision to remain in Hyde Park.

[17]Board of Trustees, *Transactions,* June 27, 1956, p. 1073. Trustees' Papers.

any money for such a campus in its 1955 budget request, and both were defeated.

Meanwhile, a major step had been taken in the appointment of the University's new president, David Dodds Henry. One of David Henry's earliest acts, even before he officially became president, was to visit Navy Pier on June 26, 1955. President Henry publicly favored the establishment of a permanent home for the two-year Chicago undergraduate division and study of the future transformation of the two-year campus into a four-year campus.[18] In August he indicated that he favored Miller Meadows as the site of the new campus.[19]

Finally, one of Lloyd Morey's last official statements as president was to strongly support a Chicago campus to a skeptical constituency. In a statement made in late August 1955, he urged the "faculty and townspeople alike [in Champaign-Urbana to] put aside local prejudices and ambition" to support a Chicago campus of the University of Illinois. Otherwise, he said, he feared a "separate school establishment under separate controls" and the "uncoordinated development of other public institutions in Illinois" in response to a "tidal wave of students in the next 20 years."[20]

With that envoi the stage was set for the new president, who took office on September 1, 1955. Much of the groundwork for a decision had been laid. The time for decision and action had arrived.

[18]*Chicago Tribune*, June 27, 1955.

[19]David Dodds Henry, letter dated August 17, 1955. UICC Archives, series 3/1/1, Box 8, Miller Meadows Site, May 1955 to June 1956.

[20]*Champaign-Urbana News Gazette*, August 22, 1955.

CHAPTER 4
Trial and Error

If we miss now, others may fill the vacuum—a municipal institution, the private colleges, branches of other state universities.

> David Dodds Henry, memorandum of May 26, 1959,
> "State of the University" (collected statements and
> memoranda), p. 327, UIUC Archives.

DAVID HENRY'S FIRST MONTHS in office were devoted to getting acquainted with the Chicago-campus location issue among others facing him as president, to reviewing earlier work done on this issue, and to beginning more detailed planning. In a meeting at the start of his term, he and Charles Havens agreed that establishment of the Chicago Undergraduate Division on a permanent basis was the University's number one project.[1] Internal planning was begun to develop an academic program for a new campus, to define building and space needs for the program, and to set target dates and a schedule for acquiring the site and completing various phases of construction. Such detailed planning was necessary not only for internal use but also as a firm basis for future legislative proposals and public support of the University.

As a basis for strategy, President Henry decided to initially seek a strong consensus for a permanent campus with a two-year program, leaving the question of a four-year program open for later development. He felt that it would not be possible to secure agreement on a four-year program in 1955 but that it would be possible to get agreement on a two-year program that could be used as a basis for a new campus. This would moderate the worries of Senator Peters and other downstate leaders as well as the private universities in Chicago. It would then be possible to ask the state legislature to budget funds for the new permanent campus and to ask for a bond issue in 1958 that would also require legislative and popular approval. Henry anticipated that over time, as the postwar babies reached college age and

[1]Charles Havens, memorandum for the file recording conversation at a meeting between himself and David Henry that, judging by the context, must have taken place soon after Henry took office. UICC Archives, series 3/1/1, box 5, "Expansion, Future Development: General, 1953–57."

clamored for entry, the need for and pressures in support of a four-year campus would become stronger and more obvious and that the change-over from a two-year to a four-year program would follow naturally.[2] (This tactic of a step-by-step process, of getting agreement on a first stage while giving time a chance to develop the pressures needed to move toward desired future directions, was one that President Henry used effectively throughout the entire effort for the new campus.)

This strategy was summarized in a March 1956 internal Havens memo which stated: "The objective is to relocate the present two-year program now offered at the Pier. However, it is vital in long-term planning to procure enough ground to take care of two or three times the students planned for in the first phase and to progress to a four-year school when and if there is a need for such. . . . The facilities . . . for the first phase of the two-year program [are] for an enrollment capacity of 8,000 FTE day students . . . [but] for long-range planning purposes, it is thought that the enrollment might reach 15,000 and the need would call for a four-year program. . . . Facilities, adequate to permit vacating the leased space at Navy Pier, shall be available for use not later than September, 1963."[3]

These assumptions were embodied in an April 1956 progress report to President Henry from the Committee on Future Development of the Chicago Undergraduate Division, which had been charged with preparing estimates of space and facilities required for a new site, developing a time schedule from 1957 to 1963, and preparing budget estimates for the 1957–59 biennium with a September 1 deadline. "The committee is proceeding with the above," the report noted, "on the assumption that G. A. Miller Meadows, or a portion of it, will be available." It pointed out that the committee could proceed on this assumption "without further assurance concerning the availability of the site" until about June 1, 1956, but that to start actual campus-plan studies would require further assurance. It was unnecessary to add that the University itself had not formally selected this or any other site.[4]

[2]David Dodds Henry to author, February 28, 1978. Author's papers.

[3]Draft of memo by C.S. Havens for internal use only, March 28, 1956. UICC Archives, series 3/1/1, box 5, "Expansion, Future Development: General, 1953–57."

[4]Havens, draft, March 19, 1956. Ibid.

At about the same time, the committee had completed a survey of the relationship between the physical characteristics and academic programs of six major urban colleges or universities as a guide for the proposed Chicago campus in relation to their academic programs. This survey examined, among other factors, enrollments, schedules, time-use of space, physical education and ROTC programs, housing needs of faculty and students, space requirements for parking, and student study and lounge facilities. It found among these schools wide differences in land acreage, but it also found general and strong agreement against the use of high-rise buildings except where absolutely necessary. High-rise structures had greater capital costs, greater operation and maintenance costs, less usable internal floor space, internal traffic problems, and a "detrimental effect upon students' attitudes toward the education program and the administration" because of the congestion and delay associated with high-rises.[5] In general, the results seemed to support, or were not inconsistent with, the University's prior thinking concerning the land acreage required (about 130 or 140 acres at the minimum), space use, and building type.

President Henry had expressed support for a permanent Chicago-area campus even before he had assumed office, and he had indicated his preference for the Miller Meadows site. His first nine months in office reinforced his earlier judgment. He was convinced that Chicago, with its large population, should have an urban campus. He had taken a key roll in establishing such a campus in Detroit, and he was well acquainted with the urban system in New York City. But, apart from Chicago's need, he was strongly aware of the great importance of a Chicago campus for the future of the University he headed. If the University did not establish a campus in Chicago, he was convinced by statements made and feelers extended that some other organization—either another part of the state system or the city itself—would construct a public university there. The establishment of such an independent, attractive, well-financed campus in Chicago would threaten the prime position of the University of Illinois in graduate and professional education in the state.

[5]Committee on Future Development of Chicago Undergraduate Division, "Conclusions Concerning Survey of Urban Universities," April 3, 1956, p. 5. UIUC Archives.

The competition for funds and for new programs that characterized the legislative discussions of budgets for state universities was then becoming more intense. In the past the University's position had been secure; its requests had been supported by both Chicago and down-state legislators. But the new regional universities had fragmented downstate support; and if another institution were to set up a Chicago campus, Chicago support, which was then uncertain, would be further threatened. The University's establishment of a Chicago-area campus would bring the support of Chicago's political leaders to the University in the legislative conflict, which had intensified as a result of the increasing competition. In the short run, the Champaign-Urbana campus might suffer diversion of some resources to Chicago that it might otherwise expect to receive; but even this diversion would be hypothetical rather than real in a period when total University enrollment would be rising rapidly and total funds available to Urbana would be doing the same. In the long run, President Henry foresaw that the Urbana and Chicago campuses together would be getting significantly more funding than would the Urbana campus alone and that the Urbana campus would be better protected from attacks by other institutions.

Of the sites under consideration, he regarded Miller Meadows the best: on grounds of its low cost, location in the direction of future population growth in the Chicago area, attractiveness of area for prospective faculty, and availability of a large amount of land that might be needed for future expansion. Henry saw the campus as an institution for the centuries, and he wished to assure space for growth and change not only in foreseeable but also in unforeseeable directions. Charles Havens, director of physical planning for the University and one of the main agents of the administration on the matter of the new campus, never saw a university that had enough space, and of the potential sites Miller Meadows qualified best in this respect.

Various members of the Board of Trustees had earlier indicated favorable attitudes toward the Miller Meadows site, and Wayne Johnston had extended feelers on the matter. On May 22, 1956, acting as a committee of the whole, the board informally discussed sites and decided to support Miller Meadows. This was confirmed at the next formal meeting of the Board of Trustees on June 27 at which the board unanimously voted "that steps be taken for the acquisition of the G. A. Miller Meadows as the permanent site for the Chicago Undergraduate Division."[6] Miller Meadows conformed to the board's desires: it had all the advantages pointed out earlier; and it would permit the creation of a green, low-rise campus attractive to potential student drivers from the suburbs and from Chicago. This campus would be like that in Urbana, but it would also make allowance for a student body consisting largely of commuters. The board members were aware of possible difficulties with the Forest Preserve District, but they felt confident that the University could either persuade the district to transfer the land voluntarily (as it had done in a few other instances) or that, if need be, with Governor Stratton's support it had sufficient influence in the state legislature to win over the district there. In addition, one of the board members thought there was a good chance for a large private grant from one of Chicago's leading businessmen for the construction of a campus at Miller Meadows.

As was expected, the University's site decision was received coldly by Dan Ryan, who was concurrently serving as chairman of both the Cook County Board of Commissioners and the Board of the Forest Preserve Commission (the two boards are the same). Ryan stated that he would follow the advice of the Forest Preserve District Advisory Commission on this matter, but he added that he would not personally oppose the University in the legislature. Possibly even more disquieting because it was unexpected was a letter to President Henry from Chester Davis,[7] a former trustee and a major figure in the Alumni Association, one of the authors of the association report supporting a suburban Chicago-area campus, and currently assistant secretary of the Army in Washington. Davis expressed opposition to the use of Forest Preserve District land for the campus site on the principle that a forest preserve should not be diverted to other uses.

In expectation that the Miller Meadows site would be available, the University asked that $2 million be appropriated in its budget for land acquisition and planning of that site. However, in response to a request from the University's Board of Trustees, the secretary of the board of the Forest Preserve Commission replied that the Forest

[6]Board of Trustees, *Transactions,* June 27, 1956, pp. 1072–75. Trustees' Papers.

[7]Davis to Henry, June 29, 1956. Johnston Papers, 119/43, vol. 1.

Preserve District would not voluntarily sell the site to the University, this on the advice of its Advisory Committee headed by Edward Eagle Brown and including Chester Davis as one of its members. This response also reflected the position of Forest Preserve District Superintendent Charles Sauers, an influential and respected official with twenty-eight years of service on the board, who felt that forest preserve land should never be alienated. Dan Ryan had no intention of acting contrary to the urgings of such powerful backers. For the University to get the land over such opposition would require that Mayor Daley be persuaded to exert strong political pressure upon Ryan and the Cook County Board on behalf of the transfer or that the matter go to the legislature for special legislation, for which the mayor's support would be essential.

Unfortunately for the University's chances within the legislature, its main Republican supporter, Senator Peters, was still against a Chicago-area campus. Without his active support, the chances of the University's winning new legislation even with Mayor Daley's support would be questionable. If the University did win over Peters's opposition, the long-run costs could be high if his friendship for and influence on behalf of the University were reduced.

There is no evidence that Mayor Daley either supported the Miller Meadows site himself or was prepared to use his influence to persuade others to support it. The mayor had discussed this site in 1955 with Wayne Johnston and was then described as being noncommittal. In early 1957, when President Henry met with the mayor and Dan Ryan to present them with and get their support for a University plan to exchange land with the Forest Preserve District, the mayor was equally noncommittal. One participant in several meetings with the mayor on this matter described him as "Buddha-like."[8] The University's legislative representatives at that time, who were taking the pulse of the legislature, felt that those Chicago legislators who were under the mayor's influence did not favor the University's position and did everything they could to oppose it short of taking a public stand. At that time, too, the mayor, shortly after his first election to that post, did not have the political strength he would acquire later; and it is

[8]Someone who has seen Mayor Daley in other contexts informs me that, when he did not wish to be drawn out or was not ready to deal with an issue, he adopted this "Buddha-like" stance.

unlikely that he would have wished to jeopardize his political capital by putting pressure on Dan Ryan to change his mind. Ryan had significant party strength of his own, and he also had the support of leading businessmen in his opposition to this site. The mayor hoped to win the support of those businessmen for his political future. In addition, he respected the legal independence of such bodies as the Forest Preserve District and did not readily seek to influence them. Finally, and probably most important, it is doubtful that he would have favored a suburban location at that time. All his advisors on urban planning are convinced that the mayor always favored a city campus and opposed a suburban campus. While the mayor's opinion on the exact site was flexible, responding to different situations, it will be recalled that as early as 1945 he had introduced legislation in the state Senate for a city campus.

In light of the absence of support from two key figures controlling legislative votes and funds and of public opposition stirred up by active efforts of the Forest Preserve District, the University decided in early 1957 that it would not seek special legislation to force the sale of Miller Meadows to it.[9] At about the same time, the potential private grantor withdrew any possibility of an offer on the ostensible grounds of adverse business.In spite of its decision, however, the University still tried to persuade the Forest Preserve District to exchange Miller Meadows for other land; and it also indicated its willingness to accept only 140 acres instead of 300. When this new offer met with no response by mid-1957, it was clear that Miller Meadows was unavailable. Evidence of this loss is the actual 1957–

---

[9]This interpretation of the fight over Miller Meadows is different from that in Edward Banfield's *Political Influence* (New York: Free Press, 1961), ch. 6. Banfield argues in effect that the University was forced over its own doubts to seem to make an effort to establish a Chicago-area campus. Miller Meadows was chosen as the site because it was unlikely that it would be available, which the University knew beforehand. I would argue otherwise. The University was committed to a Chicago campus, and President Henry's task was to establish one. The University selected Miller Meadows because it best met the Board of Trustees and the Pier faculty's picture of a desirable campus. It also thought it had enough prestige to get the site. However, it overestimated its own political strength vis-à-vis the Forest Preserve District, and it had not lined up the support of such key political figures as Mayor Daley and Senator Peters that would have been crucial in a legislative battle. The latter factor, especially, influenced the University's decision; and, in my opinion, it made the correct decision: not to go to the legislature, even though it was urged to do so and might have won after a costly battle.

59 biennium budget for a permanent Chicago Undergraduate Division. Rather than the $2 million originally requested, it allowed only $950,000, of which $575,000 was for land purchase and the remainder for planning. This alteration could permit some action but not much.

During this same legislative session, two bills were introduced: one in the House, by Paul Randolph, to appropriate $4 million for land acquisition and planning for a campus in Chicago; the other in the Senate directing establishment of a campus in Cook County with programs similar to those in Urbana. The Board of Trustees of the University opposed both bills for several reasons. While it had probably lost Miller Meadows, it did not wish to be rushed into another commitment without further thought. In part, it still favored a suburban rather than urban campus, and it was also unwilling to accept direction on programs by legislative act.[10]

In response to a protest to the board from the Parents' Association of the Pier over this opposition to a Chicago campus, Mr. Bissell, a board member, stated: "No available site within the city limits of Chicago will meet criteria of Board and long range objectives. . . . A skyscraper university would be expensive to build and to operate, [it would take] many years to acquire a site through slum clearance—[it would be] costly in funds and time."[11]

At Governor Stratton's urging, the legislature passed a bill in 1957 authorizing a $248 million bond issue, including $86 million for the University of Illinois, of which an estimated $35 million was for a permanent Chicago-area campus. The bond issue was to come up for voter approval in the 1958 election. This was the first tentative commitment by the state to such a campus, although no site had yet been chosen. The University considered this action a major step forward. The passing of this bond issue by the voters would permit the major initial capital-construction costs of the new campus to be incurred without adversely affecting funds for the Urbana campus.

[10]But, significantly, while expressing opposition to the Randolph Bill, the Board of Trustees stated that it favored a four-year branch in Chicago "as soon as it finds this expansion is necessary, and as soon as the money is available." Board of Trustees, statement re House Bill 611, April 30, 1957. UICC Archives.

[11]See Board of Trustees, *Minutes,* April 18, 1957. Trustees' Papers.

During the discussion of the University's effort to acquire Miller Meadows there were interesting reactions from those opposing the site or suggesting other sites. There was substantial opposition from inhabitants of the suburbs in the vicinity of Miller Meadows, who felt the way of life of their neighborhoods would be undermined by the influx of many students from Chicago, and they feared higher taxes associated with increased costs to them from the University's presence. While the University hoped for a relatively affluent student body in large part deriving from the suburbs, residents in the affected suburbs feared an influx of black and ethnic minorities, although few would publicly say so.

There was also opposition from elements within the city that favored an inner-city site. The Forest Preserve District sponsored a study by a city consulting firm, DeLeuw, Cather & Co., which concluded in its report of January 1957 that the Miller Meadows site was not the best available: a near-west-side site north of the Medical Center across the Congress Expressway was preferable on grounds of lower transportation cost, a more truly urban type of university, and the stabilizing effect of such a project for the neighborhood. This report spoke of the difficulties of land clearance and relocation as primarily short-run disadvantages. Since this firm was believed to favor such a near-west location before the study was started, the conclusion was not unexpected, but the arguments would be heard later.

Perhaps more important as a harbinger of the future was an informal meeting held on February 7, 1957, between several members of the Chicago Central Area Committee and C. S. Havens, which was followed by a meeting of the committee on February 20, 1957, to discuss the site. This was a private committee, the purpose of which was to build up and strengthen the central Loop area. It included top officials from such influential Loop firms as Chicago Title and Trust, Marshall Field, Harris Trust, Illinois Bell, and Carson Pirie Scott among others, as well as Illinois Central represented by Wayne Johnston. The committee formally discussed the University site for the first time at the February 20 meeting. Even though Johnston explained the reason for the choice of Miller Meadows and still expressed optimism for the possibility of getting 150 acres there, the committee voted to ask the Real Estate Research Corporation to make a study of the feasibility of locating the campus in the South Terminal area or in a blighted area in the inner city.[12]

As a follow-up to this meeting, on May 1, 1957, members of the Central Area Committee other than Wayne Johnston suggested that the University consider three inner-city sites: (1) 60 acres in the Fort Dearborn project on the Chicago River on the near North Side, (2) 45 acres using air rights over the Illinois Central Railroad tracks east of Michigan Avenue and north of Randolph Street, and (3) 65 acres using terminal land in the South Loop area from Congress Street to Roosevelt Road between the Chicago River and Clark Street. The committee argued that the University campus, in a central area site, would serve as an anchor to the Loop and protect it against continued deterioration moving from the outer edges toward the center. Such a site would help to preserve the Loop's core of over 300 acres while allowing for some expansion, thereby making it attractive for firms to remain in the Loop rather than going to other areas. It would help save the Loop by contributing to its rebuilding rather than abandoment. President Henry acknowledged the report of the committee on May 2, pointing out that the University had already considered and eliminated the first two suggested sites before selecting Miller Meadows, but that the rail-terminal site had not been considered.[13]

The University was still publicly committed to Miller Meadows and opposed a Loop location, although other sites were being proposed. A Garfield Park site was being urged by residents of that area. On June 10, 1957, the *Chicago Tribune* editorially favored a site in or near the Loop and opposed the Miller Meadows site with this remark: "Miller Meadows' only apparent advantages are a slowly moving stream and more grass and leaves."

Other issues with respect to a city site had surfaced in a November 1956 statement by the Illinois Higher Education Commission in which the private colleges were especially influential. This commis-

---

[12]See C. S. Havens to President Henry, February 11, 1957, on his informal meeting with committee members; W. Johnston's memo of February 20 on the formal committee meeting. Johnston Papers, 119/43, vol 2.

[13]Holman Pettibone, chairman of Central Area Committee, to President Henry, May 1, 1957 (Johnston Papers, ibid.); and H. M. McBain, chairman of the board, Marshall Field & Co., statement dated May 2, 1957, presenting Central Area Committee's proposals and the arguments behind them (ibid.).

sion, which was considered an opponent of the Miller Meadows site, favored a move of the Chicago Undergraduate Division from the Pier. However, at that time it opposed a four-year program, arguing that the facilities of the private institutions were under-utilized and should not be duplicated. In addition, it suggested to the University's Board of Trustees that "no night courses [be given] at Chicago" and "no residence halls" be built.[14] Those suggestions to the board are important as a record of the bargaining conditions of the private schools concerning the new campus.

The University, while continuing to announce Miller Meadows as its choice, had inevitably begun to consider alternatives. In an internal memo dated April 1, 1957, Charles Havens suggested Gage Farm, a city-owned site located at Cermak and Harlem on the outskirts of Chicago, as the best alternative to an inner-city site. The Committee on Future Development, in internal polls of faculty and staff at the Pier taken in May and July, informally ranked Miller Meadows as the best site but unavailable and Riverside Golf Club and Gage Farm in the suburbs as preferable: among the city sites, an island in Lake Michigan ranked highest, with inner-city sites ranked much lower.[15]

However, while the University continued to prefer a suburban site, whether in or out of the city, one of its most important legislative supporters was quoted, perhaps facetiously, in favor of a downtown Chicago site. Senator Peters was reported as favoring a downtown site because, he said: "I don't see any football fields downtown. If it is part of Miller Meadows they will get the whole works."[16] But whether facetious or not, this too stated a condition implicit in the negotiations between the University and a Champaign-Urbana group that opposed a Chicago-area campus.

One of the most important results of the struggle over the Miller Meadows site the University favored but lost and over the bills

[14]Statement dated November 9, 1956, UICC Archives, series 3/1/1, "Future Development: General"; *Champaign-Urbana News Gazette,* January 30, 1957.

[15]See C. S. Havens, "Memorandum Concerning Selection of Site for the Relocation of the Chicago Undergraduate Division," April 1, 1957 (draft); also Committee on Future Development of Chicago Undergraduate Division (C.U.D.): "Comparative Analyses of Alternative Site C.U.D.," May 27, 1957, and "Comparative Rating of Alternate Sites C.U.D.," July 10, 1957. UICC Archives, series 3/1/1.

[16]*Champaign-Urbana News Gazette,* July 31, 1957.

concerning a site the University opposed and actively worked to defeat in the legislature was a lesson learned by President Henry. On July 17, 1957, two years after becoming president, he wrote to Wayne Johnston: "The more I think about this the more I am convinced that, since we are bound pretty largely by what the Mayor will help us do, we had better start with him and stay with him in our planning."[17] Thus, the mayor had moved from a peripheral role to a major but still supporting role in the University's search for a site. With respect to actual funding, while the University did not get what it originally asked for, the legislature appropriated about half the amount requested and approved a bond issue that contained a large initial sum for the construction of a permanent Chicago-area campus. The state government thereby made its first substantial commitment to a new campus, although this position was weakened by the fact that the bond issue depended upon a state vote and the lack of a site would weaken popular support for it.

With the end of the legislative session and the summer vacation period, the situation was quiet until September. Then President Henry, acting on his insight, wrote to Mayor Daley expressing the University's interest in the availability of Gage Farm. While part of this site was occupied by the Municipal Tuberculosis Sanitorium, that installation would not be affected by the University's plans.[18] This letter was followed up with a visit to the mayor by the Board of Trustees' General Policy Committee and President Henry.

The mayor replied soon afterward with the nomination of Ira J. Bach, commissioner of city planning, to work with the University on the matter of site location; but, significantly, he said nothing about the Gage Farm site.[19]When, in a rapid follow-up to this letter, Havens met with Bach, there was again no mention made of Gage Farm until Havens brought it up on leaving. Instead Bach was interested in Haven's opinion of the Terminal site suggested by the Chicago Central Area Committee. He stated at the start, "Mayor Daley definitely believes that, if possible, a site should be found . . . within the City, and which is acceptable to the university."

[17]Johnston Papers, 119/43, vol. 2.

[18]Henry to Daley, September 9, 1957, ibid.

[19]Daley to Henry, September 23, 1957, ibid.

Havens pointed out that the original amount of land suggested by the committee was inadequate and that he would have to know the approximate cost and date of availability for construction. He seriously doubted that the Terminal site would be available soon enough for the completion of construction by 1963. Bach told Havens he would try to get the desired information. A continued exchange of correspondence ensued between Bach and Havens in October 1957, and Bach indicated other alternatives, such as Riverview Park and the area north of the Medical Center.[20]

In late October, Wayne Johnston received a call from James Cunningham, chairman of the Railroad Terminal Authority, again inquiring "how seriously the University is considering the area discussed [by Havens and Bach]." Johnston replied that he still favored Miller Meadows but that the University was looking at alternate sites, including the Terminal. Cunningham, like Bach, stressed the mayor's interest in a city location. Johnston replied that there were questions of sufficiency of land, the timetable, and cost that would have to be resolved before that particular site could be seriously considered. Johnston pointed out, "There must be a relationship between the cost of this area to the University and the cost of the Miller Meadows area or another area which we had in mind in the vicinity of Miller Meadows." Cunningham thought the questions could be resolved and felt sure "that he could pledge to the University satisfactory financial assistance for acquiring the area."[21]

Johnston then raised with the Board of Trustees' General Policy Committee the question of whether the University should continue trying for a site in the suburbs or settle for a site in Chicago. He still favored Miller Meadows but recognized that this could not be acquired without legislation. If that step was excluded, the University could proceed to condemn the Riverside Golf Club next to Miller Meadows; but if that site was unsatisfactory, the choice was limited to a location within the city. In that case he felt the Terminal site discussed by Bach and Havens was probably best, if the questions of

[20]Havens to Henry, September 30, 1957, ibid.; Bach and Havens correspondence of October 21, 25, 29, 1957. UICC Archives, series 3/1/1, box 8, "Railroad Terminal Site."

[21]Johnston to Board of Trustees, General Policy Committee, "Late Developments, Chicago Campus of the University of Illinois," October 28, 1957. (Johnston Papers, 119/43, vol. 2.) Later quotations in this paragraph are from the same memorandum.

space, time, and financial assistance from the city could be satisfactorily resolved.

President Henry and the members of the General Policy Committee of the board met again with the mayor in early November. The University representatives pointed out to the mayor the problems associated with the Terminal site and sought his reaction to the Gage Park site and a suburban site. While there is no follow-up to that meeting in the form of an internal memo, the *Chicago American* subsequently quoted Mayor Daley as favoring a city location for the campus. As possible sites he mentioned the Rail Terminal and the area north of the Congress Expressway opposite the Medical Center (which had surfaced as early as President Stoddard), but he made it clear that the final choice was up to the Board of Trustees. (Interestingly, on the previous day the *Chicago Daily News* had reported that the Miller Meadows location was definitely out. The same article stated that the trustees preferred a campus that would not be surrounded by deteriorated properties and that the neighborhood problems of the University of Chicago and the Illinois Institute of Technology were lessons for the University of Illinois.)[22]

In order to permit careful consideration of the Terminal and other possible city sites as well as suburban sites, the Board of Trustees in March 1958 requested the Real Estate Research Corporation to carry out, for completion by September 1958, another study of possible sites for a permanent Chicago Undergraduate Campus. The proposed timetable of University action called for selection of a site and budgeting of funds for the 1959–61 budget biennium during the 1959 legislative session ending June 20, 1959, if construction was to be started in 1959 or 1960 in time for completion of the first stage by 1963. (This assumed success of the bond issue in the 1958 election.) While the site study was to set out criteria to be used in selection and to catalog all possible sites, only a few sites were to be studied in depth—two of these were the Riverside Golf Club in the suburbs and the Terminal site in the city. With respect to these two sites, the Real Estate Research Corporation would carry out preliminary architectural and engineering studies, including transpisation analyses, so as to make possible detailed estimates of cost and a feasible timetable

---

[22]*Chicago American,* November 23, 1957; *Chicago Daily News,* November 22, 1957.

for construction. In its directions for this study, the University, although recognizing the initial stage as the transfer of the Pier's two-year program to a permanent site, seemed more direct than previously in stating the likelihood of a four-year campus at a later date.

One of the most serious problems of the University administration at this time was the loss of confidence among the faculty and students at the Pier. Havens, who had been working closely with Pier administration and faculty and had their confidence, felt a strong suspicion concerning the seriousness of the University's intention to establish a permanent Chicago undergraduate campus. This suspicion was caused by:

1. The delay in acquiring a site and starting construction.
2. The strongly expressed opposition by many members of the academic staff at the Urbana-Champaign campus.
3. The strongly expressed opposition by the local [i.e., Champaign-Urbana] legislators toward any permanently constructed facilities in the Chicago area.
4. The decision on the part of the University not to adopt an aggressive program to acquire Miller Meadow[s].
5. Lack of a well planned and executed program of public relations.

The University administrators to whom Havens sent this memo agreed with his analyses of attitudes at the Pier but disagreed as to the desirability or value of a public relations program "under circumstances which force us to be less than candid in our public statements on some points and to await decisions from a variety of politically motivated public officials."[23] The only means of dispelling these suspicions would be to produce results and not public relations; meanwhile, the administration could only wait out the suspicion.

The Real Estate Research Corporation presented its report to the

[23]See Havens to Ray, March 18, 1958; Dangerfield memo, March 25, 1958; Ray to Havens, April 4, 1958. (UICC Archives, box 7, "Expansion—Site Selection, March 1958 to March 1961.") It was about this same time that Banfield was collecting material for his study of decision-making on the issue of a Chicago campus. While he interviewed Pier officials and faculty, he did not interview Urbana administrators; and this suspicion of Urbana pervades the picture he paints. It is possible, too, that city and county officials interviewed by him were then interested in placing responsibility for the Miller Meadows failure with the University.

Board of Trustees and the public on October 23, 1958.[24] The criteria
were not dissimilar to those used in the earlier report: accessibility to
50 percent of the potential students from Cook and DuPage counties
by public transportation and to at least 85 percent of potential students
by car within forty-five minutes; availability that would permit construction to start by mid-1960; a two-year program for 6,000 students
to start by 1963 and a four-year program for at least 15,000 students
by 1965; expandability above minimum acreage preferred; lower-
cost sites preferred over higher-cost sites; and those with superior
enviroment (defined to include such factors as physical condition and
safety, proximity to job opportunities for students, and housing for
faculty) preferred.

Using these criteria the report ruled out urban-clearance sites
"which would require the demolition of a large number of dwelling
units immediately" on grounds that the difficulty of relocating people
on top of the existing backlog would be insurmountable within the
University's time schedule.

> Any attempt to clear an area rapidly for the University would seriously
> disrupt . . . other programs already underway. To satisfy this crite-
> rion, therefore, land sufficient for the 6,000 student campus must be
> mostly vacant and readily available. However, it is possible that the
> acquisition of the additional area needed for the 15,000 student cam-
> pus could be accomplished through residential clearance:
>   1. If a minimum possible number of families were involved.
>   2. If the amount of relocation in any one year would be so small
>   as not to have a major effect on other programs.[25]

In all, 83 sites were cataloged, including numerous clearance
areas, two of which were the Harrison-Halsted and adjacent clearance sites. All clearance areas were ruled out, and four sites that did
not call for extensive clearance were considered outstanding and
were examined in further detail. The latter were the Riverside Golf
Club (next to Miller Meadows), Northerly Island on which Meigs
Field is located, the Rail Terminal area south of the Loop, and

[24]Real Estate Research Corp., "Analysis of Sites for Campus of the Chicago Undergraduate
Division, University of Illinois," multilithed (n.p.: Real Estate Research Corp., 1958), pp.
1–23 for summary. UICC Archives, box 6.

[25]Ibid., p. 8.

56 Decision-Making Chicago-Style

Garfield Park. Those sites averaged about 130 acres each in size, of which about 35 acres could be used for parking. In addition, the quoted criteria concerning the ruled-out clearance areas were of interest, since they in fact seem to permit the later consideration of what would be the partially cleared Harrison-Halsted site after the four preferred sites were eliminated during the succeeding two years.

Between the board's receipt of this report in late October 1958 and the next board meeting, two major changes occurred as a result of the November 1958 election. The bond issue for funds including those for the University of Illinois's new proposed campus did not receive a majority of the popular vote as required, although it had the support of the governor and most downstate legislators. Three Republican board members, including the chairman, Park Livingston, were defeated in the election by their Democratic challengers, so the board majority shifted to become Democratic. The new members would formally join the board in March 1959. In addition, in August 1958, shortly before the Real Estate Research Corporation's report was received, Chicago's Department of City Planning issued its "Development Plan for the Central Area of Chicago." This recommended construction of the new campus of the University in an area south of Congress and east of the Chicago River, which the department hoped would be released by consolidation of the rail terminals south of the Loop. (This same plan included the Harrison-Halsted project, covering 55 acres, for residential and some commercial development.[26] This had by then been approved by the city and federal governments, and funds had been allocated for it.)

The consequences of these three events outside the University were of major importance in the continuing process of choosing a site. The defeat of the bond issue, which had received a majority of the votes cast but not the number required, because many voters did not vote on the issue, meant the University would again need legislative action for funds for a Chicago-area campus either by appropriation from current revenues or by a vote for another bond issue in the 1960 election. For either option the support of Chicago legislators would be vital. In addition, if there was a referendum on a new bond

[26]Department of City Planning, *Development Plan for the Central Area of Chicago* (Chicago: City of Chicago, 1958), pp. 7–8, 19–21, 31–32.

issue, active support of the Cook County Democratic organization would be essential in the general election to override the deficiency in downstate support that had led to the defeat of the bond issue in 1958. (In fact, with more people voting in the presidential election of 1960, the amount of effort expended would also have to be greater.)

While the Board of Trustees carried on its discussions in a nonpartisan manner, the election of a Democratic board was important, because the new board majority was probably somewhat more sympathetic than the old one to a city site. This was indicated in remarks made by the newly elected members concerning the site recommendations in the Real Estate Research Corporation report, when in February 1959 they were nonvoting guests at the last meeting of the old board at which the report was acted upon.

Finally, the inclusion of the campus in the Central Area Plan for the city signaled the mayor's preference for the South Loop Railway Terminal site and his intention to work for it as a goal of his administration.

The period from November 1958 to March 1959 was a time of transition and of key decisions in this process. Although a new board had been elected and would take office in March, it was considered essential for the University's budget preparation for the 1959 session of the legislature that a site decision be made before March, so the University could prepare its request for funds to acquire land and plan on that site. The General Policy Committee of the board, in preparing its site recommendations for the board's February 19, 1959, meeting, sought information from the mayor on the Terminal site, but this was unavailable. Wayne Johnston, who was very knowledgeable about that area as a result of his position as president of the Illinois Central, was very doubtful that any plan releasing that land acceptable to the railroads could be worked out to meet the University's construction timetable. There were also the questions of availability of Garfield Park from the Park District and of the environment around the Park. Statements of opposition to the use of Northerly Island (Meigs Field) as a site were issued by the Chicago Association of Commerce and Industry and were also expressed by the city's newspapers.

On the basis of those considerations and after hearing expressions of preference for the Meigs Field site from the members-to-be, the General Policy Committee recommended and the old board, in its last meeting, agreed that the Northerly Island and Riverside Golf Club sites should be given first priority. The Railway Terminal and Garfield Park sites were excluded on grounds of uncertain availability, high cost, and comparatively poor neighborhood environment. Of the two preferred sites, the committee concluded that, although there was strong sentiment for a city location, "since the Committee has no assurance that Northerly Island is available, or that it will be made available within a reasonable time schedule, or at a cost equal to or less than that projected for Riverside, the Committee believes the Riverside Golf Club should be designated as the site since it can be acquired through proceedings in eminent domain, if necessary." However, the committee also recommended that if Northerly Island were made available to the University within thirty days, "at a reasonable cost compared to that projected for the Riverside Golf Club," this action should be reconsidered.[27]

This action by the board selecting a suburban site precipitated decisive action on the part of Mayor Daley to persuade the University to choose a site within the city. On February 23 the mayor met with President Henry and the Board of Trustees and requested a delay in action on the site until about April 15, when the engineers' report on the rail-consolidation study would be available. More important, he concluded that "because of the great opportunity the University would offer the people of Chicago, the city would be willing to defray any extraordinary costs which would arise out of the selection of a site in Chicago."[28] The board acceded to his request. President Henry immediately directed University officials involved in budget preparations that "the administration will . . . assume the amount required for Riverside would be the base need."[29] In effect the city had now agreed to make up the difference between the estimated cost of approximately $4.3 million to acquire land and carry out planning for

[27]Board of Trustees, *Minutes,* February 19, 1959, pp. 287–92. Trustees' Papers. It is somewhat difficult to explain the board's action, except as showing a strong belief in the desirability of a suburban site. By this time the political difficulties of achieving such a site were clear. It may, however, also have been an effort to force the mayor's hand toward a city site; it certainly had that result.

[28]Richard J. Daley to Board of Trustees, statement, February 23, 1959. UICC Archives, box 8, "Railroad Terminal Site."

[29]Henry to Farber, University comptroller, February 24, 1959. Johnston Papers, 119/43/4, box 9.

a campus at Riverside Golf Club and the cost of a site within Chicago for the same purposes. The University could consider the price of land in both places equal.

In addition to this commitment from Mayor Daley, the state legislature at Governor Stratton's strong urging passed a second bond-issue bill in 1959[30] to replace the one rejected by the state in 1958. This bond-issue bill, to be voted on in the November 1960 elections, asked for $195 million for the six state universities. It included $50 million to be used for a Chicago campus of the University of Illinois and $25 million for a new campus at Edwardsville for Southern Illinois University (which amount was inserted at the same time as the amount for Chicago). This new bond issue, which, as we shall see, passed in the 1960 election, was a key element in the entire process. It provided the first massive capital funding for the campus, and it did that without impinging on funds for the future of the Urbana campus.

Governor Stratton's role in initiating both the 1958 and 1960 bond issues was obviously of major importance. The inclusion of funds for the new Southern Illinois University campus in the 1960 bond issue helped achieve the essential support of the southern tier of the state, and support of the Urbana community and alumni was achieved once it became clear that the new campus "was not being built at the expense of the Urbana campus."[31] The legislation for the bond issue must have received support from Senator Peters. He had probably been convinced by President Henry and other University representatives of the desirability of a University of Illinois campus in Chicago on the grounds I outlined earlier; and the bond issue convinced him that such a campus could be financed without harm to his Urbana constituency. Unlike the situation when Miller Meadows failed, the elements of a successful political coalition in favor of a Chicago campus were in place: Governor Stratton had always supported the campus and now favored a city site; Mayor Daley strongly supported the campus, since he knew it would be in Chicago; and Senator Peters accepted the campus, as did other downstate legislators, once it was

---

[30]A significant interest group urging this bond issue upon the governor and legislature was composed of leaders and legislators from the Garfield Park community who strongly favored the campus.

[31]Henry to author, February 28, 1978, Author's Papers. Dr. Henry stressed the great importance of this 1960 bond issue and Governor Stratton's major role in it.

realized that institutions in other parts of the state would not be weakened by a bond issue which also gave them funds. But the Chicago site still had not been selected; and unless the University and city administrators could reach agreement on a site, there would be no new University of Illinois campus in Chicago.

A Site Is Chosen

. . . chieftains do not debate their positions endlessly. . . . They settle for what works in
the human condition and neither long for nor seek perfect solutions. . . . In an imperfect
world [the chief] does what has to be done, forging compromises and less than ideal
solutions constantly.

> Eugene Kennedy, *Himself! The Life and Times of Richard
> J. Daley* (New York: Viking Press, 1978), pp. xiii–xiv.

MAYOR DALEY'S STATEMENT to the University in February 1959, in which he offered to pay the extraordinary costs of land acquisition within the city beyond the costs of a surburban site, changed the conditions of negotiation between Chicago and the University. Until that offer was made, the University was taking the initiative on the site selection, and its preference had been for a "green" site, one with abundant land and expansion possibilities. A suburban site at a low price had been the first choice, and the only site of the desired character within the city had been Northerly Island (Meigs Field). But the city's offer made possible broader limits to the search than the suburbs and Meigs Field; money would now be available for other sites at a higher per-acre price. But the initiative had changed. It was now up to the city to make available the land upon which the University could build a campus of adequate size— ultimately for 20,000 students—within the University's time schedule. Failure on the part of the University to agree to a site the mayor might propose could jeopardize its ability to raise funds for any other site and its ability to acquire funds for other purposes in the future, both in the legislature and by bond issue.

The key figure for the city in making the site decision would be Mayor Daley. Combining within himself the chief political position in the city as chairman of the Cook County Democratic Central Committee and the city's chief administrative position as mayor, he was the most important political figure in the city. In addition, he saw his role as much more a leader than had his predecessor, Mayor Kennelly. From his first speech as mayor, he had made it clear to the City Council and the city that he would use his political and administrative powers to lead rather than follow. But in the early days of his tenure as mayor, during the period when the campus decision was being made, he did not have the dominance he was to acquire later. Then there were important party figures, such as Dan Ryan and Jack Arvey, he might not wish to alienate, because he needed their future support; and, too, he had to consider the theoretically independent agencies, such as the Forest Preserve District and the Park District, that had their own points of view as well as control over substantial patronage.

Apart from his relationship with these political figures and agencies, Mayor Daley, from the start of his first term, sought to build up a close relationship with the Loop business community. When he defeated Mayor Kennelly in the party primary and then Robert Merriam in the general election in 1955, the leaders of the Loop business community and the newspapers feared that he might bring back machine rule and corruption, so he did not have wide support. But, by his intimate knowledge of the city's finances, his establishment of control over the City Council, his willingness to listen to the business leaders, and, above all, by his leadership and initiative in a great rebuilding program for the Loop and the city, with its associated beneficial tax policies and bond issues, he won political and financial support.

The business community's Central Area Committee saw the proposed campus as an important element in its effort to preserve and strengthen the Loop, and the city administration's proposal of the Central Area Plan in 1958 followed up that committee's suggestion that the campus be placed in the terminal area south of the Loop. When the mayor ran in his first campaign for reelection in May 1959, that plan, as well as the mayor's offer of help to fund the land-acquisition costs of a city camqus in early 1959, must have been strongly influenced by his political needs both then and in the longer run. This was inevitable not only in 1959 but also later. It was important for him to have the continued support of business, and loss of the campus to the suburbs could have had costly political consequences.[1]

[1]For a picture of Mayor Daley's political situation at the time of the decision, as well as of his political methods and biography, I found the following books useful: William F. Gleason, *Daley of Chicago* (New York: Simon & Schuster, 1970), especially pp. 223–28, 278–84, and 337–40; Kennedy, *Himself!*; Milton Rakove, *Don't Make No Waves—Don't Back No Losers* (Bloomington: Indiana University Press, 1975), especially, pp. 82–89 and 186–90; Mike

But while the mayor obviously preferred to have business support, he could not control the actions of the business community. He could not force private railroad companies to sell their land and terminals to the city for a campus, and neither the city nor the University could exercise the right of eminent domain over railroad land. Similarly, he could not force independent agencies, such as the Park District, to make their land available to the city or to the University for any other purpose except at a political cost. Thus, while he could urge a preferred site or veto an undesirable one, he himself could not select a site unless the city already owned the land. Also, he had made a commitment to contribute if necessary to the purchase price of land for the campus. He would have to find funds for this by shifting the funds for such purpose from some other other purpose, by finding additional city revenues, or by shifting the burden to some other level of government—state or federal, or a combination of these.[2]

While the mayor always had to be conscious of the political reasons for and cost of his actions, his interest in establishing a public university in Chicago preceded his mayoralty and transcended politics. He had an underlying belief, based on his own experience, that the children of workers' families should have a chance to go to college. He considered education one of the most important means of economic and social improvement. His father had been a business agent in the Sheet Metal Workers' Union, and his mother had strongly encouraged his own efforts to reach an important position by completing studies in a private college and law school, which he had done while working. He felt others should have the same opportunity but at a public institution. The trade unions of the city, with which he had close emotional and political ties, strongly supported a city campus for similar reasons, quite apart from any jobs the construction might promise. The mayor's feeling for the value of education com-

---

Royko, *Boss* (New York: New American Library, 1971). An internal memorandum of a conversation, dated July 13, 1962, summarizing an exchange between a high city official and a representative of the University, refers to the political importance of construction of the campus for the 1963 mayoral election. "Congress Circle Campus: Acquisition of Site," Legal Counsel's Office, UIUC.

[2]The mayor's success in achieving this shift in general was stressed in H. Woods Bowman, "Paying Big City Bills," a paper delivered at an economics seminar at UICC on November 30, 1977.

bined with a strong personal belief in Chicago and in the need to preserve the Loop as a key to stemming threatened deterioration of the city. He personally supported the efforts of business firms to stay in the Loop, and he felt that public policy should do the same. By his highway construction program, he sought to stimulate traffic into the Loop. He felt that siting of the University campus should also be used, if possible, to protect and anchor the Loop.[3]

In addition to this feeling for Chicago and the Loop, the mayor had a strong "gut" belief in the city's neighborhood character. In remarks made in 1955 when he was first sworn in as mayor, he had described Chicago as "a city of neighborhoods," adding: "I have lived all my life in a neighborhood of Chicago—all that I am I owe to the influence of my family, our neighborhood and our city. . . . I resolve to be the mayor of all the neighborhoods—of all people of Chicago."[4] As we shall see in the site decision, his often-expressed faith in the value of a neighborhood would be challenged by his support for public higher education in the city, and the latter would win out.

The immediate consequence of the mayor's offer of funds was to postpone action by the University's Board of Trustees, and it eventually resulted in the board's dropping its effort to acquire Riverside Golf Club for the campus. The decision was postponed several times to await the results of negotiations with the railroads. During this period strong opposition to the University's selection of the golf course built up. Opposing the site were the Riverside community which feared a change in its character, the Riverside legislators, the major Chicago papers, the Chicago Federation of Labor, the Chicago Real Estate Board, the Chicago City Club (which preferred the railroad terminal but suggested as an alternative an area on the near west side of the Congress Expressway across from the Medical Center),[5] and leading Chicago Democratic state legislators, some of

[3]Walter Netsch has pointed out to me, as an example of the mayor's concern and use of public policy to strengthen the Loop, the priority he gave to the Kennedy, Ryan, and Eisenhower expressways, all of which move traffic *to* the Loop; whereas the proposed Crosstown Expressway, which was intended to divert traffic *from* the Loop, was given a lower priority. Interview, October 11, 1977, Author's Papers.

[4]Kennedy, *Himself!* p. 133.

[5]For the City Club position, see "City Club Opposes U. of I. Site," *Real Estate Adviser*, March 6, 1959.

whom indicated they would have difficulty in supporting appropriations for a suburban site.

Apart from the inhabitants of Riverside, who were mainly interested in *not* having the campus there, the other groups *favored* a city site, either at the Rail Terminal or Garfield Park. On April 21, 1959, the state House of Representatives, responding to the groups favoring a city site and strongly urged by the residents of Garfield Park who felt they had such a site, voted disapproval of a surburban site and urged the trustees to locate the campus within Chicago.

Havens, in a memo to President Henry, which the president forwarded to the board on May 1, 1959, stressed the need for a decision by June 1959 at the latest if the campus was to be ready for 8,000 students in 1964 and almost 20,000 students in 1969. At that time Havens considered Meigs Field the best site: it offered a possibility of unlimited expansion by building additional land into the lake, a desirable atmosphere with an assured integrity (i.e., it could not be affected by the enviroment), and a dramatic quality. But any of the three city possibilities—Meigs Field, the Rail Terminal, or Garfield Park—was acceptable if the site could be made available in time to meet the University's time schedule, i.e., if it was available by July 1960 and if certain conditions specific to each site were met. Caveny, in a supporting memo, stressed the importance of keeping to the 1963 schedule.[6]

But Meigs Field was eliminated by the mayor, ostensibly on the basis of a report on that site dated May 15 made by Ira Bach at the request of the University. This report pointed out: (1) that the city had made arrangements with the Park District for the lease of Northerly Island and with the Federal Aviation Agency for use of the Island as an airport for twenty years or more, (2) that serious transportation problems would be associated with the use of the Island for a campus, and (3) that building a new island for the campus would be very expensive and time-consuming. Bach therefore recommended that

[6]See Henry to Board of Trustees, May 1, 1959, stressing need to act by May 16, 1959, with supporting memos from Havens and Caveny (Johnston Papers, 119/43, vol. 4). Havens, looking back at his recommendation in retrospect (interview, April 7, 1978, Author's Papers), said he no longer felt that Meigs Field was as good a site as he had then thought it to be; transportation would have been very much of a problem. Plans for these sites were prepared by Skidmore, Owings & Merrill. (See Appendix B.)

Meigs Field not be considered further. The mayor accepted his conclusions and informed President Henry accordingly. In effect Bach's study supported the previously expressed opposition of leading business firms in the Loop, the city's newspapers, and Park District officials to the Meigs Field site. Clearly the mayor was unwilling to override those groups.[7]

This left the Garfield Park and Rail Terminal sites. On May 6, 1959, the mayor had asked the Board of Trustees to continue considering the Rail Terminal area, with Garfield Park to be considered as an alternate if the Terminal area could not be made available by April 1960. The trustees, however, felt this delay was not possible, and on May 16 they voted that Garfield Park was the preferred site provided certain conditions could be met and the cost to the University did not exceed that of the Riverside site. They recommended that steps be taken to begin transfer of the land to the University, and that enabling legislation for this be sponsored by the Park District and the city. The board also urged that the governor request and the General Assembly vote for funds to be used for land acquisition and that the proposed University bond issue be amended to increase its total by $50 million to be used for the construction of buildings and purchase of equipment for the new campus. The board also stated that it would rescind its February decision on Riverside as soon as the acquisition of Garfield Park had been assured.[8]

President Henry wrote Mayor Daley and the president of the Park District informing them of this action and asking the city and Park District to sponsor any legislation required for conveyance. The letter to the mayor also asked his support for the amended bond issue. The mayor replied that he would support such legislation but that he would continue to inform the board of progress on the Rail Terminal site. But these actions were partly for insurance and partly for bar-

---

[7]See Johnston Papers, 119/43/5, May 15, 1959, for the Bach report. I was told that Northwestern University spokesmen also strongly opposed that site, but I have found nothing in the files to confirm this. Also, Meigs Field had been named after the publisher of the *Chicago American,* the only newspaper to support Daley for mayor in 1955. Meigs and his paper strongly opposed use of the field by the University, a fact that may have influenced the mayor.

[8]See Board of Trustees, Committee on General Policy, "Report on Site Selection for Relocation of the Chicago Undergraduate Division," May 16, 1959. UICC Archives, series 3/1/1, box 8, "Garfield Park."

gaining purposes; they were not a decision. The University felt that Garfield Park was the site likely to be available in time to meet its schedule for the opening of a new campus in 1963 or 1964 and therefore requested that action be started on this. Although the mayor preferred the Terminal site, he would, more or less as insurance, permit the start of action that would be required to make the Garfield Park site available.

The Garfield Park–Austin community—homeowners, business-men, the area newspaper (*The Garfieldian*), community groups, and political leaders—strongly favored location of the campus in Garfield Park. The president of Sears, Roebuck, which had facilities on the West Side, wrote the mayor in March 1959 favoring the Garfield Park site. Representative William G. Clark, who represented the area in the legislature and was a leader on the Democratic side in support of Paul Randolph's efforts to locate the campus in the city, also urged the Garfield Park location. That support had been conveyed to Gov-ernor Stratton, who was sympathetic, and it would contibute to the legislature's approval of the new bond issue later in the year.

It was felt that siting of the campus in Garfield Park would stabilize property values there and encourage families to retain their homes. At that time a major transition was beginning in the area. The area east of the Park had already experienced a massive influx of blacks, some of them migrants into the city, but far more of them relocated from other parts of the city where their homes had been destroyed by city highway and redevelopment programs. The residents west of the Park hoped that placing the campus in the Park would reduce the impetus of the black movement into the area, both by serving as a barrier and by attracting upper-income and professional residents from the University, thereby maintaining or raising land values. The net effect would be to conserve the existing community and halt the threatened deterioration. This was the only community in any of the sites considered that actively sought the campus.

While the community itself supported the campus, many other groups in the city opposed a Garfield Park campus. Conservationists, such as members of the Audubon Society and Carl Condit, noted architectural historian of the city, opposed the sale of park land. Perhaps of more importance to the mayor was the opposition of James Gately, president of the Park District, who had earlier opposed giving up any part of the Park; and of Colonel Arvey, probably the most influential figure on the Park District Board and Daley's predecessor as leader of the Democratic party in Chicago, who was still influential in the party and opposed the sale vehemently in private meetings with University officials. The opposition of both men was based on their belief in the value of a large park to the city; and they were opposed to any change in Garfield Park, such as building a campus and replacing the park land with a network of smaller parks as suggested by the University.

But a substantial group within the city still favored the Terminal site. This group included influential businessmen in or near the Loop who were represented in the Central Area Committee, the Metropolitan Housing and Planning Council, the Marshall Field newspapers, and the *Chicago American*. In May 1959 the Metropolitan Housing and Planning Council sponsored the organization of the Joint Action Committee of Civic Organizations (JAC) to work for the location of the campus in the Rail Terminal area. The new organization was headed by Andrew Boemi of the Madison Bank and included some of the leading Loop business and professional organizations, as well as such nonbusiness groups as the CIO trade union council and the Chicago branch of the NAACP. The committee was well staffed with members from the Metropolitan Council, notably Dorothy Rubel; and it had ready access to leading political figures in the state and the city as well as to the newspapers. Apart from favoring the Terminal site, it opposed the Garfield Park site vigorously as being less preferable on two grounds: (1) that it should remain a park, and (2) that in such an area the proposed campus would soon be faced with the same problems confronting the University of Chicago in Hyde Park. The JAC threatened a series of suits that would indefinitely prevent transfer of the park land. Since much of the land had been given to the Park District by specific deeds for park use only, serious legal problems might ensue if it was not used for this purpose. Thus the JAC threat could pose a real obstacle to the University in meeting its timetable.[9]

But, most important, the mayor always preferred the Terminal site;

[9]See Joint Action Committee, 1959–61 news releases and statements to the Board of Trustees, Governor Stratton, Mayor Daley, and others. UICC Archives, Dorothy Rubel Papers.

while never publicly opposing Garfield Park, he clearly never considered it other than second best. The reasons for the mayor's refusal to
support Garfield Park are obscure but may have arisen from a combination of elements: his own strong attachment to the Loop and
its preservation, and the strong support given the Terminal site by
most of the Loop's leading business firms and by the large city
newspapers; the opposition of Park District board members, with
their patronage, to the sale of park land to the University, and his
respect for both the district's independence and its opinion; strong
opposition within the district, notably on the part of Colonel Arvey,
to the sale of the Park, and the mayor's reluctance to fight him on such
an issue at that time; and, finally, the civic opposition to the loss of
park land.

Although the Terminal site was preferred by the mayor and by
many who opposed the Garfield Park site, the University administration and Board of Trustees were well acquainted with the difficulties
involved in the effort to consolidate the terminals south of the Loop
and possibly move the incoming lines to a terminal elsewhere.
Wayne Johnston's Illinois Central Railroad was deeply involved in
those negotiations.[10] Although Johnston had been optimistic about a
possible consolidation when Cunningham had first raised the matter
with him in late 1957, this was no longer the case. While engineers
made proposals, the railroads were unwilling to accept them, and the
city could not condemn their land.

The railroads were asking far more for the land and for construction of a new terminal than the city was prepared to pay. The
minimum figure mentioned in the newspapers was $40 million; and
Johnston, in private communications, estimated the total cost of a
feasible plan at closer to $140 million. In addition to the high price the
city was being asked to pay for the land, the railroads were also
unwilling to sign expensive long-term leases for the use of a new
terminal when they already had very inexpensive leases for the use of
the old terminals and were pessimistic about long-term trends in

[10]In fact, early in 1959 one of the new trustees suggested that Johnston abstain from
participating in the General Policy Committee when the Terminal site was discussed, to avoid
any suspicion of conflict of interest. However, other board members unanimously supported his
participation, and the suggestion was withdrawn. See Johnston Papers, 119/43/4, April 16,
1959.

passenger travel. As support for this, Johnston reported that Colonel Crown, the major stockholder in the Rock Island Railroad, said that the Rock Island would not move from its LaSalle Street terminal to the crowded quarters of Union Station and that he (Crown) did not expect a consolidated passenger terminal in Chicago within the next ten years.[11] Some of the railroads, such as the Illinois Central, wanted their own terminal in the area to continue to be used after the consolidation.

The whole structure of ownership and lease rights in the old terminals was highly complex, and it seemed to outside observers that there was little advantage to the railroads in a move at that time. Because most of the concerned railroads had headquarters elsewhere, negotiations with them were a lengthy and time-consuming process in which a minority of the railroads had a veto. The differences between the city and the railroads remained so wide that the mayor himself never felt the matter was worth his time and prestige to participate.[12] As negotiations dragged on, Johnston reminded the board members that the first proposal for consolidation of the South Loop terminals had been made before World War I, that nothing had happened then, and that he did not expect rapid results at this time.[13] (This is the same area currently being considered for the Chicago 21 Plan, and a new stadium has also been proposed for the area. In the years since 1959 the land has remained undeveloped, while rail traffic has declined.) But the city remained somewhat more optimistic: the site remained the mayor's first choice, and the newspapers and the Joint Action Committee continued to support it. Pressure was brought to bear on the University to delay its timetable. City officials made statements to that effect to the newspapers, business groups

[11]Johnston Papers, 119/43/5, box 9: Johnston to Henry, December 7, 1959; Johnston to Trissal, December 29, 1959.

[12]Author's Papers: interview (November 19, 1977) with Dean Swartzel, head of the regional HFA office in Chicago at that time, and with Paul Gapp (September 26, 1977), now architecture editor for the *Chicago Tribune* but then on the staff of the *Chicago Daily News.*

[13]In fact, Daniel Burnham's famous Plan of Chicago (1909) suggested consolidation of the railroad terminals and abandonment of trackage between the Loop and Twelfth Street. See Perry Duis, *Chicago: Creating New Traditions* (Chicago: Chicago Historical Society, 1976), p. 52. For a short history of the various terminals, the numerous efforts to consolidate them, and the present status of the Terminal area, see Perry Duis and Glen Holt, "The South Loop Legacy," *Chicago* 27 (September 1978):238–40.

questioned the urgency of the need for the campus, and some newspapers editorialized for delay.

But with no action occurring and in the face of projections for continued increases in enrollment, the University representatives felt strongly that the schedule must be maintained. President Henry, in his State of the University address for 1959, stressed the need for keeping to a timetable that would permit the new campus to open in 1963 or 1964 at latest. As one site after another was ruled out and the city and Park District dragged their heels on Garfield Park while favoring the Rail Terminal, Henry painted a gloomy picture of progress in a memo for the record that also revealed his fears and motivations. He pointed out that the negotiations on Garfield Park were discouraging and remarked that everyone with influence in the city—developers and central-area businessmen—wanted the Terminal site in the South Loop. He wrote:

> Even more serious is the chance of losing the opportunity for action. At this point, all parties are committed to move. . . . A year from now any one of them may be an obstacle to unified action.
>
> I have the feeling, too pessimistic perhaps, that if we do not settle now on Garfield Park, we shall not have a site in Chicago for another ten years, if ever.
>
> If we miss now, others may fill the vacuum.[14]

For the University the most encouraging as well as important event of this period was the action taken by the state legislature shortly before adjournment on June 30, 1959, passing the amended bond-issue bill proposed by Governor Stratton, which contained the $50 million requested by the University for a Chicago campus. But the bill would still have to be approved by the voters of the state in the 1960 elections. Everyone was aware that this would call for a major effort on the part of the University and other interested groups to avoid a repetition of the 1958 loss.

The legislature had also appropriated $2.5 million in new funds for land purchase, planning, and site preparation, in addition to reappropriating the unspent money legislated in the previous session, bringing to $3.3 million the amount available for those purposes in

---

[14]David Dodds Henry, "State of the University," p. 327, memorandum dated May 26, 1959, UIUC Archives.

the 1959–61 period. With these funds the University could carry on planning and site-development work that would permit it to start building in 1961, to open a new campus with a two-year program in fall 1963, to add a third year to its program in 1964, and to have a full four-year program by 1965. But this timetable depended upon the city's making a site available by September 1959, and a delay in that decision would delay the opening for a year. The legislature had also passed the bill that would make possible the transfer of land from the Park District to the University for a Garfield Park campus. In July 1959, however, Havens was still uncertain of the mayor's position on Garfield Park, the relation of the Park District to the University's request, and the legal availability of the land in Garfield Park to the University; and there still was no certainty that funds would be available for construction in the 1961–63 biennium. Havens pointed out that if the city did not make its decision by September 1959, the University might consider whether (1) to reopen its efforts to get the Riverside Golf Club by condemnation to meet its 1963 timetable or (2) to expand the campus in Urbana and give up the idea of a permanent campus in Chicago. In fact, these alternatives were not feasible then, and the University continued to wait beyond the September 1959 deadline for a city decision; but it also began to think about establishing an undergraduate college south of Florida Avenue in Champaign-Urbana.[15]

The University contracted with Skidmore, Owings & Merrill for extensive planning studies using Garfield Park as the prospective campus site. But as of late November 1959, the city still had not made a firm offer of Garfield Park; its first choice still remained the Terminal area. But should the Terminal site be unavailable, it appeared to the University that Garfield Park would be made available; in fact, a procedure to test the legal issues in the transfer of Garfield Park to the University had been agreed upon between the University, the Park District, and the city *without in any way committing any of the parties concerned to the release or purchase of the land.* It was hoped that this would permit a court decision on the

[15]See Havens to Henry, July 2, 1959, Johnston Papers, 119/43/9; and "Report Concerning Site Selection and Time Schedule to Relocate the Chicago Undergraduate Division," September 11, 1959, UICC Archives, series 3/1/1. Interview with Norman Parker, former UICC chancellor, December 14, 1977, Author's Papers.

matter by early 1960, but a delay by the Park District set back that possibility.[16]

Without informing the University, the city administration itself had begun to consider at least one site alternative to Garfield Park if the Terminal site proved unavailable. Phil Doyle, executive director of the Land Clearance Commission, had early in 1959 informally brought the 55-acre Harrison-Halsted clearance area first to the attention of the City Plan Commission and then the mayor as a possible site for the campus. While this area had been committed for housing redevelopment, no developer had yet committed himself to the area. Doyle was aware of the problems with the other sites which were not under the city's control; he knew, too, that the city already had title to some of the land in the Harrison-Halsted area for a residential land-clearance project, and he thought the city could still get substantial federal funding for that area plus a surrounding area if the proposed use were changed from residential to university use. He also believed strongly that a campus in that area would serve as an anchor for redevelopment of the near West Side east of the Medical Center and that it was a good central location for a public university. However, when he first raised the possibility, there was no response, because other sites were being considered and the area had already been committed for other uses. But by late 1959 the other sites still had not become available. The Harrison-Halsted idea surfaced again at the end of that year during a trip made to Washington by the mayor and his urban advisers, Ira Bach, Phil Doyle, and D. E. Mackelmann. Either they suggested it to the mayor after discussing the site problem among themselves and he accepted the idea or the mayor recalled his earlier conversation with Doyle and now expressed interest in the idea. In any event he asked Ira Bach and the City Plan Commission to begin the spade work for such consideration but directed that this be done quietly, without informing the public or the University until an internal decision had been reached.[17]

[16]Havens to Caveny, November 19, 1959, on planning for relocation of the C.U.D, UICC Archives, box 8, "Garfield Park." Johnston Papers, 119/43/9: Henry to Daley, November 2, 1959; Havens to Henry, November 27, 1959.

[17]The story of this trip is based upon memories of advisers who had made it almost twenty years earlier (Author's Papers: interview with Ira Bach, September 29, 1977; D. E. Mackelman, October 25, 1977; and Phil Doyle, November 10, 1977). Although memory of details was

Meanwhile, wheels continued to turn on the Garfield Park and South Loop sites. At its December 15, 1959, meeting the University's Board of Trustees reiterated that "since no negotiable proposals . . . have been received in regard to the Rail Terminal site, its availability to meet the University's time schedule, or as to its cost, the University has proceeded with its planning for use of the Garfield Park site. . . . [That] site appears to be the only site on which construction can be completed by the fall of 1963 for occupancy of a new campus. . . . Even on this site prompt action will be required by the [City and the Park District] if this time schedule is to be realized."[18]

It was obvious however, that the city preferred the Terminal site. Interested businessmen and newspapers continued to exert pressure on the city and the University to get and use that site, and they urged the University to delay making a decision until it became available. A *Sun-Times* article of November 24, 1959, concerning existing urban campuses referred to Wayne State as having only 63 acres (the approximate size of the more available part of the Terminal area). President Henry remembered that Wayne had a much larger area. He wrote to the president of Wayne State and asked for specific information, referring to this article as "part of the editorial slant to squeeze us into a Loop site."[19]

At this point the University could do little except urge speed on the

---

fuzzy and sometimes contradictory, there was agreement on the important point that the idea had been raised and the mayor had asked for action. See also A. Rotstein, "The Circle Campus: The Site Was the Ball Game" (Master's thesis, University of Chicago, 1971), pp. 38–40.

Florence Scala has pointed out that Phil Doyle was meeting often to discuss plans with area residents and the Hull-House Community Participation Committee at that time. The committee had identified a potential developer, Mr. Stastny; and in 1959 much work had proceeded on plans for housing, including architectural styles. Apparently Alderman D'Arco and a group of residents were also working on plans and had identified a developer, to whom the Land Clearance Commission was reluctant to offer the land. Author's Papers: interviews with Florence Scala and Ernest Giovangelo, October 26, November 16, December 5, 1977.

[18]Havens to Parker et al., December 17, 1959, with copy of the board's action on December 16, UICC Archives, box 8, "Garfield Park."

[19]Henry to President Hilberry of Wayne State, November 1959, ibid., box 9, "Expansion: Urban Universities." The University was determined not to be squeezed into a smaller area than it felt desirable; and that was at least 130 acres. The Santa Fe Railroad was supposedly prepared to offer 30 acres in the Terminal area free of charge to the city; but the spokesman for the city said the University would never accept such an acreage, so the offer never got any further. Interview with Charles Genther, UICC faculty, March 9, 1978, Author's Papers.

city and do its own planning while waiting for the city to act. The need for action was supported by a December report of a Legislative Commission to Visit State Institutions that found an acute emergency at the Navy Pier campus and urged an immediate final decision on a permanent site. As nothing happened, the morale of students and faculty at the Pier fell, and the students mounted demonstrations in the mayor's office to urge action on a site.

President Henry continued to take steps to reduce opposition from the city's private colleges to a new public campus. As late as March 1959 the president of Loyola University had written to the mayor and President Henry opposing a city campus, especially a central-area campus, favoring instead a state scholarship program for the private schools. That summer President Henry wrote a letter to the presidents of the major colleges and universities in the city and stated: "The University of Illinois has no plans for the development of evening school work in connection with the development of the Chicago Undergraduate Division." He also indicated that, while he could not make commitments for his successors or subsequent Boards of Trustees, "should the University be expected at some time in the future to offer its services in the evening, we would be interested in doing so only in a way not to conflict with the services of the other institutions in the Chicago area."[20] This action reduced or eliminated a politically potent source of opposition to the campus that city officials considered important.

The University agreed, thus, that there would be no dormitories, football stadium, and evening school at the new campus in the near future. Also, little graduate work was anticipated in the next few years while a faculty was being assembled, although the University in its program planning allowed for some graduate programs by 1970 and for facilities for graduate faculty programs and research in the future. These statements disarmed most of the academic opposition to the new campus both from the city's private colleges and from the University's Urbana campus. In any event, the obvious crush of new students made the need for a Chicago campus clear, and the effort of outside groups was directed toward trying to control the development

[20]Henry to John T. Rettaliata, president of I.I.T., July 30, 1959, and to other college and university presidents as well as Ben Willis, superintendent of schools in Chicago. Johnston Papers.

of that campus in a way that would avoid long-term threats to their interests.

However, in any documents concerning future plans for the new campus, President Henry was very careful to avoid making any statements that might seem to bind his successors. He felt that during its first five or ten years, the Chicago campus would be fully occupied with getting its new four-year undergraduate program staffed and underway, and little would be lost by these limitations. But for the long run, detailed prediction of future directions was not possible, and limits were therefore undesirable. The important thing was to start the campus under the University's auspices under conditions that would permit long-term development in any direction that was considered appropriate to future needs by the University's future administrators. A university was an institution for centuries and not for decades. The University of Illinois was not only planning the physical elements of a new campus on an undetermined site; it was also carrying out, under the lead of Norman Parker, the program planning that would determine which buildings would be required and the timetable for their construction.

At a meeting held on December 15, 1959, the Board of Trustees favored Garfield Park as its choice. Mayor Daley again met with University officials on December 21, and afterward announced through the *Garfieldian* that another railroad consolidation report had been prepared. But the announcement continued, "if the railroads do not fully accept this plan within a reasonable time, or if the University, after studying it, decides that it still prefers to go ahead with the Garfield Park site, the city will then cooperate to build the campus in Garfield Park." At this meeting with the University, the mayor also stressed for the first time that "consolidation of the rail terminal facilities and selection of the site for the Chicago [campus] were two separate and distinct projects." Of the two, he was clearly less optimistic about the rail terminal consolidation project.

Havens pointed out in a follow-up memo that the University would have to study both sites in detail. Such studies on the Terminal site and any negotiations with respect to both that site and the Garfield Park site would take about two months; only after their completion could the University reach its decision.[21] In fact, the new engineering

[21]*Garfieldian*, December 22, 1959. Havens to Henry, December 24, 1959, UICC Archives and Author's Papers.

Aerial view looking north (February 1961), showing the Chicago Circle (upper right) and the near West Side area with precampus structures framed by Congress (top), Roosevelt (bottom), and Halsted (right); the diagonal street is Blue Island. UICC ARCHIVES.

Aerial view looking east (August 1964), showing the near West Side area with campus structures in proximity to the Chicago Circle (left center), Navy Pier and the Loop (upper center), the Jane Addams housing project (lower left-center), and the South Loop Railway Terminal area (upper right-center). UICC ARCHIVES.

The Hull-House building complex circa 1951. WALLACE KIRKLAND

The razing of Hull-House (1963). UICC ARCHIVES.

Hull-House and the residents' dining hall after restoration (1964) with University buildings in the background. uicc archives.

studies on the Terminal site did not answer University needs for data, and the new consolidation plan for the area was clearly unsatisfactory. In a meeting held on February 24, 1960, the board's Committee on General Policy reported that the Rail Terminal site was not a feasible choice, and it recommended that a proposal be made to the city and the Park District to acquire the Garfield Park site. The board accepted this recommendation on March 16, 1960.

At about the same time, the mayor stated to the newspapers that he and the University were prepared to wait for a year before reaching a final site decision.[22] On that date, however, President Henry wrote the mayor, informed him of the board's March 16 action ruling out the Terminal site, and submitted the proposal to acquire Garfield Park at a cost to the University equal to the price of Riverside Golf Club, with the city making up the difference. He asked that the city and Park District act on the proposal within a month.[23] In April, action to test the legality of the General Assembly Act of 1959, giving the Park District the right to convey Garfield Park to the University, was begun as a friendly suit filed before Judge Harrington in the Circuit Court of Cook County. Chicago newspapers, the *Daily News, Sun-Times,* and *American,* all questioned the University's rejection of the Terminal site. In addition, the Joint Action Committee opposed the decision to acquire Garfield Park and entered the case as an intervenor to prevent sale of the land by the Park District. This was done even though by this time the railroads had rejected consolidation plans for the terminals in the area and discussions were clearly at an impasse.[24]

Meanwhile, behind-the-scenes movement was proceeding in city offices on the Harrison-Halsted Hull-House site. At the meeting of the Hull-House Board of Trustees held on December 18, 1959, James Downs, a member of the board, spoke in favor of a possible Hull-House sponsored cooperative housing program in the area. But at the board's meeting of April 28, 1960, Downs, who had become board chairman, brought to the board's attention a newspaper article which reported "that [the] Hull-House Land Clearance area and some adjacent land might be offered to the University of Illinois as the Chicago

[22]*Chicago Tribune,* March 17, 1960.

[23]Henry to Daley, March 16, 1960, Johnston Papers, box 9.

[24]See Board of Trustees, *Minutes,* April 20, 1960 (Trustees' Papers); *Daily News, American,* and *Sun-Times,* March 23, 1960; *Daily News,* March 24, March 30, April 12, April 15, 1960; *Tribune,* March 29, 1960.

site for the University in an attempt to reach a compromise between the Garfield Park location and the Railroad Site." This possibility had been discussed at a special meeting of the board's executive committee held the previous week, since it would clearly impinge upon future planning for Hull-House, which might call for public fundraising for as much as $750,000 for rehabilitation of the old buildings.

But Downs felt the Hull-House board would have plenty of time to consider the matter, since no proposal had yet been made; and, in the event such a proposal was made, the Board of Trustees of the University and the Land Clearance Commission would have to agree before it could become effective. Downs would, of course, know of this, since apart from his association with Hull-House he was one of the mayor's closest advisers on urban matters and had close ties with the University as a distinguished alumnus and chairman of the Real Estate Research Corporation.[25] Perhaps most important, he felt that a decision either way was certain by July 1; and the executive committee recommended to the full board that planning for the rehabilitation of Hull-House should be slowed down until then. The full board, acting on recommendation of its executive committee, at the April 28 meeting, voted a motion that if any official proposal was made to take over the Hull-House area for the University of Illinois all pertinent information should be made available to it before a meeting at which the proposal would be fully discussed. These Hull-House board meetings were entirely confidential and nothing was said publicly about the possibility.[26]

On about May 1 the mayor formally directed the Department of City Planning to prepare a plan for the campus at the Harrison-Halsted site, but this was still internal. On May 3 Ira Bach told Charles Havens that he was studying an alternate site, but he did not disclose its location and expressed the hope that he might be able to do so soon. On May 11 the *Daily News* leaked a story with a map that the city was studying the Harrison-Halsted project as an alternate site, a story which appeared only in the first edition and was then pulled.

[25]In dealings concerning the site issue, the relationship between University officials and James Downs was kept at arm's length. Because the various roles played by Downs posed a real or suspected conflict of interest, University officials normally dealt with Richard Nelson, president of Real Estate Research Corp., and only rarely with Downs himself.

[26]Hull-House Board of Trustees, *Minutes,* April 28, 1960, Scala Papers.

In a confidential report made to the Hull-House board at its May 26, 1960, meeting, Downs reported on the status of the site studies, adding that discussions had been held between groups involved with the site (but he did not identify the groups). He said that he expected a decision would be made by June 20 and that, if the decision was made to proceed on the matter, the Hull-House board should have a proposal to discuss by the time of its meeting on June 30. However, as of June 21 the city formally advised the University only that it was studying a site of one hundred acres in the Harrison-Halsted area. It gave no other information, and no cooperation was requested. Havens asked permission of the University board, and the board agreed, to request that Skidmore, Owings & Merrill and the Real Estate Research Corporation make preliminary studies to evaluate the site from the point of view of the University before making any public comments once the city publicly announced the results of its studies if they were positive.[27]

Nothing was announced at the June 30 meeting of the Hull-House board, but at least one member raised the question of what would happen to Hull-House if the campus was built in the area. However, in another meeting of the board held during the summer, Downs reported confidentially "that within the next 2 or 3 weeks a serious proposal will come forward re the University of Illinois taking over the Harrison-Halsted Land Clearance Area as the site for its Chicago campus. When the proposal is made a board meeting will be called." He also indicated that if a proposal was made by the city to the University's board and if the board accepted, the matter would then come before the City Council and probably the state legislature, and there would then be public hearings.[28]

Meanwhile, on June 22, 1960, in year-end speeches at Navy Pier and the Medical Center, President Henry publicly stated that Garfield Park was the University's choice. The test suit on that site, however, was still pending in the Circuit Court. The Joint Action Committee continued to press for the Terminal site, but various city officials

[27]Ibid., May 26, 1960; Havens to University Board of Trustees, June 21, 1960, Johnston Papers, 119/43/5; "Informal Chronology of Events on Site Selection of University of Illinois in Chicago," p. 18, Scala Papers.

[28]Hull-House Board of Trustees, *Minutes,* n.d., but either July or August 1960, Scala Papers.

announced publicly that the issue of consolidation of the terminals was separate from that of selection of a campus site. In early July the *Sun-Times* leaked a story "that the city may recommend a Westside site unless negotiations for the railroad site are concluded by August 1. . . . The prime criteria set for the selection of a site—immediate availability and availability for students—point to 55 acres in [the] Harrison-Halsted site."[29]

In August the city's plan for the Harrison-Halsted site was finished, but it was still not made public. However, the city was aware that the newspapers knew of this site, and some announcement would have to be made shortly. Havens brought the site up specifically at the August 15 meeting of the Interim Committee to Advise on Physical Planning for the Chicago Undergraduate Division, the University's internal planning committee for the site. He anticipated that the city would present the Harrison-Halsted site to the University sometime in September, after devoting considerable time and thought to its development. He felt "the advantages are so great-. . . that it will probably be difficult for the University to objectively refuse to consider the use of this site. . . . One of the outstanding factors relating to the acceptance of this site would be that if accepted, the University and the site would receive the backing of the Mayor, the Council, the City Planning Commission [sic], and many other authorities. On the other hand, should the University decide to decline and attempt to continue with its . . . use of the Garfield Park site, it would probably find all of the above groups against it. In other words, the Garfield Park site probably will represent an up-hill battle all the way as opposed to more or less cooperation should they agree to accept the Harrison-Halsted site."[30] Havens didn't state it, but the lengthy delay in the suit over the legality of transfer of the Garfield Park land and the first decision supported his point.

On August 26, Judge Harrington ruled that the legislative act of July 1959 enabling the Park District to convey the Garfield Park land to the University was unconstitutional on various grounds and enjoined the Park District from selling the contested plots of land to the University and the University from buying those plots with public

[29]*Sun-Times,* July 6, 1960.

[30]Interim Committee, *Minutes,* August 15, 1960, pp. 4–5, UICC Archives, box 4.

funds. Both the University and the Park District appealed to the Illinois Supreme Court, with the strong support of the community. This would delay any possible action on the site for many months.

A meeting between the Board of Trustees and other officials of the University and the mayor and officials of the City Plan Commission, at which the city would formally present the Harrison-Halsted area as an alternate site, was first scheduled for September 14; but it was postponed until September 27 because of the death of Arthur Cutts Willard, a former president of the University. On September 13 the mayor announced the September 27 meeting and its purpose to the newspapers. He cited as advantages of the Harrison-Halsted site its availability and its comparatively low cost. When questioned, he stated that it was still only an alternative to the Terminal site; and he criticized the railroads for their opposition to, and delays on, consolidation. He pointed out that the Terminal site could still be used for other purposes if the terminals should subsequently be consolidated and that failure to use the site for the campus was not the end of the Central Area Plan. The mayor stressed the need "to get the University into Chicago as fast as possible" as the main reason for the suggestion of the Harrision-Halsted alternative.[31]

In preparation for the scheduled September 14 meeting with city officials, Havens sent a memo to the board alerting members to what he had been able to learn informally about the Harrison-Halsted site. In this memo he summarized what he thought were the reasons for the availability of this site: the city's inability to find a developer for the original proposed housing project and its need to have a site alternative to Garfield Park for the University. He expected that the city would try to make this site as attractive as possible to the University and that this site would probably have priority over both the Terminal and Garfield Park sites. He reported his opinion that the main disadvantage of the site was the surrounding area, which he described as "probably the most depressed area in the City." This poor environment would make development of a suitable campus more difficult and would "probably result in a completely different type of campus" from that possible at Garfield Park or Riverside. He suggested that

[31]*Daily News*, September 13, 1960; *Sun-Times*, September 14, 1960; *American*, September 15, 1960.

University officials question the mayor at the meeting but not comment on the site's desirability. However, the University should indicate willingness to study the site and to carry out such a study over a period of several months in order to decide whether to accept it or not.[32]

The mayor presented the Harrison-Halsted site to the University at the September 27 meeting in the form of a report prepared by Ira Bach and the City Plan Commission. While other sites were also ostensibly examined in this report as alternatives to the Terminal and Garfield Park sites, nearly the entire report was devoted to Harrison-Halsted, which was recommended to the University "as an excellent alternate site" which should be given "serious consideration . . . for possible development of a permanent 4-year branch . . . in Chicago."[33]

The land to be made available was 145 acres, bounded by Congress Expressway on the north; the South Expressway, Halsted, and Newberry on the east; Grenshaw, 14th Street, and Roosevelt on the south; and Blue Island and Miller on the west. At that time the Chicago Land Clearance Commission was assembling and clearing 43 acres in the Harrison-Halsted project; that acreage would be the core of 61 acres that could be made available for immediate development by June 1961. An adjoining area of 84 acres would be designated by the commission for the second stage of campus construction, to be cleared and transferred to the University by July 1963. The price of this land would be established by estimating the value of the land for the residential purposes for which it was first cleared, and it would be sold to the University at the price at which it would have sold for residential structures. In subsequent discussion it was stated that only Harrison Street, Taylor Street, and Roosevelt Road would remain open to cross the site.

Havens suggested certain questions to be asked of the mayor at the September 27 meeting concerning the city's expected efforts on this site, the availability of information from the city for the University's site studies, the status of underground utilities in the area, the city's plan for the surrounding areas, and procedures to be taken. He also

[32]Havens to Board of Trustees, September 9, 1960. Johnston Papers, 119/43/5.

[33]Ira Bach, "Presentation of Harrison-Halsted Site," September 27, 1960, mimeographed, pp. 7, 15. UICC Archives and Author's Papers.

wanted the mayor to make clear the city's willingness to pay the costs above those at the Riverside site.[34]

Following this meeting, the Chicago Plan Commission, in its meeting of October 6, 1960, formally approved a change in the Central Area Plan for the city that shifted the proposed location of the University campus from the Terminal site south of the Loop to the Harrison-Halsted area as offered at the September 27 meeting.

At the September 29 meeting of the Hull-House board, James Downs reported the mayor's offer of the Harrison-Halsted site to the University and explained that offer. He believed the University would ultimately accept the offer "on the basis that everything now in the area goes out, including Hull-House and the new Catholic school." But the University would not accept until after its bond issue had carried in the November elections and its trustees had formally accepted the site. Downs stressed that the University would have the right of condemnation if they accepted the land. "Once the deal is closed [in late 1960 or early 1961] the city will be committed to deliver all the land necessary within one year." On this basis Hull-House would have about another two years in its present location.[35]

Two questions are implicit in this review of events up to the city's offer: (1) why did the mayor decide on Harrison-Halsted, which had never been seriously considered or recommended as a site; and (2) what was the reaction of the people living in the area to its being offered to the University as an alternate site?

One can only guess at the mayor's motives. He was under great pressure from the University to select a site to meet the timetable to enroll the first flood of expected additional students. This need was constantly being stressed by the University both in private meetings with city officials and in public responses to demands for further delay until the Terminal site should become available. The University's search for a location had gone on for over five years, and there were indications that patience was wearing thin. If the University now decided not to build within the city, it would be a blow to the mayor's image as a developer and to his political future. He wanted

[34]Havens, "Questions Concerning the Harrison-Halsted Site," memorandum, September 20, 1960, ibid.

[35]Hull-House Board of Trustees, *Minutes*, September 29, 1960, Scala Papers.

the site within Chicago, and his first choice was the Terminal area. But several years of discussion had made clear that there would be no agreement reached between the railroads and the city in time to meet the University's schedule. The differences on the technical level remained so wide that there was little reason to believe that they could be bridged even by the mayor himself entering into the negotiations. The mayor preferred a site near the Loop, if a site within it or at its edge was not possible—this both on personal grounds and on the urging of many business leaders whose support was important to him. Garfield Park was four miles from State Street; in addition its use was opposed by the Park District and by powerful forces within the Democratic party, in spite of the favor shown it by its own community. Also, complex legal problems over the transfer of the land might delay the issue. Meigs Field was out of the question because of the opposition of Loop business groups and newspapers, as well as for a variety of other reasons.

On the positive side and most important, the city already controlled the land in the Harrison-Halsted area, although it had been designated for another purpose, and on it building could start immediately. Adjacent land could apparently be declared a clearance area quickly to give the University the total space it felt it needed. Thus, there was no need to appeal to other agencies for land they might be unwilling to sell. Also the area was east of the Medical Center and offered a chance for the redevelopment of the whole area between Ashland on the west to the Dan Ryan on the east. Then, too, this would relieve the mayor of much of the financial commitment he had made to the University when he had promised to pay land-acquisition costs above those of the Riverside Golf Club. Since Harrison-Halsted, unlike the alternate sites, was an urban redevelopment site, a substantial proportion of the additional cost could be shifted from the city to the federal government under the Urban Renewal Act.

Not only was there an educational need for rapid movement on the site at this time, there was also a political need. Although the mayor had won an overwhelming victory in the 1959 election, he was seriously threatened by a major police scandal in early 1960. His main rival, Benjamin Adamowski, the state's attorney for Cook County, was threatening to make this scandal a major campaign issue, both in his own campaign for re-election in 1960 and also in his expected run against Mayor Daley in 1963. It was therefore doubly important that action on the new campus proceed quickly: the site must be chosen in 1960 well before the election or the state bond issue on which so much depended might fail again, and the construction should be in process well before the 1963 election so the mayor could benefit from it in that campaign. The campus would be tangible evidence of the mayor's interest in education and in the welfare of the city's lower-income groups who would benefit from the new institution as well as of his ability to implement major redevelopment projects for the city. The location of the campus near the Loop, even though not at the unavailable Terminal site favored by many of the Loop's business leaders, would still be acceptable to those leaders whose support was important to the mayor.

Several other supposed reasons given for the choice of the Harrison-Halsted site rather than another might possibly be dismissed. Several people who might know and numerous rumors circulating in the site area at the time to explain the sudden and apparently arbitrary decision suggest that the Harrison-Halsted site offered greater possibilities than others for jobs and graft for Democratic party workers in the condemnation and clearance processes and more opportunities for hidden gains by speculative land purchases in the surrounding area. In my talks with such strong opponents of the site decision as Florence Scala and Jack Mabley, a skilled investigative reporter who would have ferreted out and publicized any hint of corruption, I have not found anyone who feels that corruption or its opportunity influenced the decision. Only one transfer of land in the project area might hint of dubious behavior to the suspicious. However, that transfer was made after the decision was made to offer the site to the University; and the new owner of that parcel of land did not favor the decision. If that transfer had any such purpose, it had the effect, rather, of repaying someone who would be adversely affected by the decision. As originally planned, the offer of land to the University had included three acres between Miller and Morgan Streets. Those three acres were removed from the offer just before the September meeting and were made available for development to a firm in which the alderman of the district was believed to have had some interest. In any event, neither he nor the firm made any profit from the land, which they no longer own.

A second suggestion mentioned is that the mayor wanted to weaken Italian political control of the area and to break the West Side bloc. But, if that was the case, why would Aldermen D'Arco and Marzullo have gone along with him at the expense of their own political futures? In any event, it did not have that effect. In my opinion the mayor selected the Harrison-Halsted site, which contradicted earlier commitments and ran counter to his belief in neighborhoods, not out of strength or a long-range, deliberate strategy, but out of an inability to offer his preferred site and an unwillingness to offer other suggested sites in what had become an emergency under the pressure of time. All other apparent possibilities for an inner-city site had been ruled out for one reason or another, and he had to offer the University something quickly or risk losing the campus to which he was publicly committed. Furthermore, unless a site was offered before the November 1960 elections, the chance of defeat of the bond issue would have been much higher, and without that money the Chicago campus would probably not have been constructed.

In retrospect, why did the community make no response to this at the time? This is especially surprising in light of the strong response made after the University's acceptance. The offer should not have been a great surprise: it had been leaked in the papers; Phil Doyle had mentioned to at least one of the area's inhabitants who worked in the Land Clearance Commission that the site was being considered; and some Hull-House staff members who lived in Hull-House were aware that the city was considering the area as a site. In fact, the Italian, Greek, and Spanish-speaking residents of the area didn't believe it could happen. They knew the fabled power of the Italian political leaders of the area and felt those leaders, who were close to the Democratic city leaders, would never agree to such a proposal which would change already committed plans for the area from residential renewal to institutional use. Then, too, they had seen many signs and efforts that had encouraged them to clean up and invest in improving their homes, and many of them had. In addition, they had recently contributed to rebuild the Holy Guardian Angel School, and Mayor Daley himself had attended its opening. Those who were more knowledgeable knew that, while a developer may not have been definitely found, several developers had expressed interest and were negotiating; and a community group had been incorporated with the intention of starting residential redevelopment. Parcels of land were to be conveyed by the Land Clearance Commission to this group so that its members could start building houses. City officials obviously knew of this and of the work under way in the area. When Father Scola, pastor of the Holy Guardian Angel Church and one of the community leaders heard the rumors, he and the alderman went to see the mayor, who told them that this was just being mentioned as a possible alternate site, that they need not worry.

Sometime later the mayor made the formal offer, which he would not have done without having first discussed it with the ward committeeman, who was also the alterman. Alderman D'Arco apparently did not like the decision, but he had little choice. According to one report the mayor had told him that he had to choose that site and that D'Arco would have to go along. The vote on this in the City Council would be a matter of party discipline, and it would pass. The mayor added that he would have no objection if the alderman himself would vote against it, as he subsequently did. The mayor supposedly sweetened the pill for the alderman by agreeing to change the western boundary of the campus from Miller to Morgan Street; and it was also supposedly understood that if the University had to expand further it would not be to the west. The area between the campus and the Medical Center would remain largely Italian, ensuring Italian political control there for the future. Thus, while the alderman probably knew of the decision, he had little choice but to go along with it.

Finally, Hull-House, which was another connection to the city establishment for another neighborhood group, knew something but said nothing. The usual connections between Hull-House and groups within the neighborhood had broken down, as we shall see later. Thus, signals to the neighborhood were either nonexistent or confusing, and the usual neighborhood leaders—priest, alderman, and Hull-House staff—gave no warning. This absence of any strong reaction from the neighborhood community in the critical interval from July 1960, when the story first leaked, to early 1961,[36] may have convinced the mayor and his staff that any community unrest

[36]There were expressions of opposition from Senator Libonati, the district's representative in Springfield, and from Father Scola after the formal offer was made in September; but at that time these were simply individual statements.

could be handled without undue problems. However, several know-ledgeable informants are convinced that the mayor expected serious difficulty and some unrest to result from the decision and that he had decided to take whatever political heat arose from it.

Whereas Hull-House was physically part of the area and its staff was normally involved in neighborhood affairs, the members of its Board of Trustees were all outsiders to the neighborhood, although not to the city, with varying degrees of interest in the neighborhood. When at the September 29, 1960, meeting Downs informed them of the city's thinking and action, the main questions of the board members revolved about the future of Hull-House—the physical and symbolic presence—rather than about the neighborhood in which it had always worked. It was pointed out at this meeting that a petition was being circulated in the neighborhood urging that Garfield Park be selected. Downs advised that "the answer of Hull-House to all in-quires about [its] position in this matter will be that so far the idea is only a proposal; and that when it becomes a definite plan the Hull-House Board will take action and make its position known."[37] There was no need to do anything until after the University had decided whether it would accept the site, and Downs promised to call a special meeting of the board to consider what its strategy would be at that time. The Hull-House board members were influential in Chicago, and their opposition at this time could have been effective; but any such possibility was successfully muted. Both the city and Universi-ty, realized, however, that Hull-House could be a strong opposing element that might have to be neutralized by concessions.

With the new site offered, the major tasks facing the University were winning the bond-issue election in November 1960 and careful-ly examining the city's offer. The University had prepared its budget for the 1961–63 biennium during the summer of 1960, before a site had been chosen; a major component of its capital budget was $42.5 million for the Chicago campus, the funds for which were to come from the bond issue.

Unlike the defeated bond issue of 1958, which combined a request for funds for institutions of higher education with those for state welfare institutions, the 1960 bond issue for higher educational

[37]Hull-House Board of Trustees, *Minutes*, September 29, 1960, Scala Papers.

institutions was separated from any other purpose. The new bill was designed for greater flexibility of allocation than the defeated bill, and its funds would be available more widely to educational institutions throughout the state. The University of Illinois mounted a major campaign to support the bill. It chose Joseph Begando, the assistant to the president (now chancellor of the University's Medical Center) to head the campaign, and Park Livingston, a former trustee (and later a member of the board), to educate the public on the issue and to develop support. Other public institutions did likewise in the face of needs created by greater enrollment. Even private institutions supported the bond issue, since they clearly could not meet the anticipated enrollment pressure themselves and could not seem indifferent to an expected demand far beyond their own capacity or intention to expand. The Illinois Agriculture Association again led the opposition on conservative fiscal grounds as it had also done in 1958. All advocates of the bill felt that the 1960 election would be more difficult than that in 1958 because it was a presidential election year. Far more people would be voting for legislative candidates than had done so in the 1958 off-year election, and the yes vote would therefore have to be larger than that required in 1958.

The Yes vote in the 1960 election substantially exceeded the necessary majority of the highest legislative vote, and the bond issue won. Compared with the 1958 vote, the difference lay in Cook County, where in 1958 the Yes vote had been barely greater than the needed majority, although it had exceeded the No vote by about 370,000 votes. This slim margin had not been sufficent to counterbalance the lower Yes vote in the rest of the state. In 1960 the Yes vote outside Cook County slightly exceeded the No vote but was still substantially below the needed majority. But within Cook County, the Yes vote was almost 500,000 above the required majority and 300% greater than the No vote. This avalanche of Yes votes in Cook County swept the bond issue in the state.

A major difference between the 1958 and 1960 election's was that in the latter election Mayor Daley had offered a Chicago site and knew the campus would be located in Chicago. While the defeat of Adamowski for state's attorney was the key local issue for the party, directions had also gone out concerning the importance of the bond issue and instructing the wards to get out the vote in its favor. The party suceeded in getting the vote out, Adamowski lost, and the bond issue won. At the same time, the massive Cook County vote won Illinois for presidential candidate John F. Kennedy and elected Otto Kerner governor. This was one of the few times in recent history that the president of the United States, the governor of Illinois, and the mayor of Chicago were simultaneously Democratic. This would ease the solution of any administrative or legislative problems connected with an urban-renewal campus site. For the first time the University had funds to build a new campus without adverse effects on the old one, and it had a definite site offered by the city. It was now up to the Board of Trustees to decide what to do about the city's offer. In anticipation of a successful end to the search for a site, President Henry, on December 21, 1960, formally appointed Norman Parker vice-president of the Chicago campus, and the organization of an administration for a full four-year campus was under way.

The period from November 1960 to January 1961 was one of study and comparison between the two sites located at Harrison-Halsted and Garfield Park. The main disadvantage of the former was found to be facilities of the Commonwealth Edison Company, including a substation, which would restrict the area for University building. While the city was prepared to move its own utilities from the area, it was not prepared to pay $15–$25 million to relocate the utility company's substation and underground power lines. This, in fact, seemed such a disadvantage to the offered site that in December 1960 President Henry and Wayne Johnston met with Don Maxwell, publisher of the *Chicago Tribune,* to ask the newspaper's support for the Garfield Park site, to which Maxwell agreed.

Another problem of the new site was solved more easily by a change in the site boundaries. The southern boundary of the site as offered in September 1960 had extended to 14th Street. This boundary was moved north to Roosevelt Road in January 1961, and in exchange the project area was given more land extending west along the Congress Expressway to Racine—some of which was planned for the University's use and some for residential high-rise construction. Several reasons apparently accounted for the change. Roosevelt Road, a major thoroughfare, would no longer cut through the campus. The distance between the new campus and the Medical Center would be shorter, and investments by hospitals in the area east of the center might be used as local matching contributions to secure a federal grant. The location south of Roosevelt Road would have dispossessed blacks who might have been more difficult to relocate than whites; it would have adversely affected the Mexican community there; and it would also have required the razing of a second Catholic Church, St. Francis, attended largely by Mexican parishioners, and would have further antagonized the Church, which was already bothered by the loss of Holy Guardian Angel Church and School. (Subsequently, when the new gym was built south of Roosevelt Road, much of the land *around* St. Francis was cleared to build it.) It was believed that reducing the conservancy area in the largely Italian Congress-Racine residential area as a result of the boundary change would cause less difficulty, and the change was made in spite of both the legal establishment of that conservancy area and a promise made to the people living there that location of the University would not reduce the conservancy area.[38]

On January 16, 1961, the Illinois Supreme Court overruled Justice Harrington's earlier decision. This new decision ruled that the Park District might sell the land in Garfield Park to the University if it wished, but that the University had no right to condemn the land if the district did not wish to sell. On the same date Johnston wrote Don Maxwell that the problem of the utility substation and its facilities had been solved by new plans for location of the University's buildings.[39] Maxwell felt that he had been misled by President Henry on this matter, and the *Tribune's* support for the Harrison-Halsted campus site was considerably weakened.

Availability of the Garfield Park site was still threatened by opposition from the Association of Commerce and Industry and by the decision of the Joint Action Committee to appeal the Illinois Supreme Court's ruling to the U.S. Supreme Court. In addition, there were continuing legal issues over the University's right, if and when it

---

[38] G. Burd, "The Role of the Press in the University's Search for a Site," 2 vols. (Ph.D. diss., Northwestern University, 1964). Author's Papers: Havens to John M. Smyth, Jr., February 27, 1961, acknowledging first boundary change made after the September 27 offer; F. W. Kraft of Skidmore, Owings & Merrill to Havens, "Advantages of the Harrison-Halsted Site," December 7, 1960.

[39] Johnston to Maxwell, January 3, 17, 1961, Johnston Papers, 119/41. Interview with David Dodds Henry, December 2, 1977, Author's Papers.

acquired the park land, to remove the limitations on those sections of the park with restricted use and over the compensation it might have to pay for that removal. Most important, however, the Park District itself had not agreed to sell, and it refused to reply to the University when questioned about this on February 9, 1961.

During this period Havens wrote several memos comparing the two prospective campus sites. The differences between them did not seem great, but the crucial difference was in the immediate availability of the Harrison-Halsted site in comparison with the Garfield Park site, which was still tied up by threatened litigation. While those memos do not again mention the city's strongly positive attitude toward the Harrison-Halsted site in preference to the Park site, it is clear that this was an underlying factor to be considered once the utility and boundary matters had been resolved. On February 10, 1961, members of the General Policy Committee of the University Board of Trustees met with the mayor to discuss the site. The February 10 issue of the *Daily News* subsequently reported that the Board of Trustees had agreed to accept the Harrison-Halsted site; but this was somewhat premature, since the committee did not report to the full board until February 15.

In its report the committee ruled out the Garfield Park site on the ground that possible litigation imposed too great a delay; the same held true in the case of the Rail Terminal site. The Harrison-Halsted site met all criteria of the board, and it was available. The committee therefore recommended to the board acceptance of the Harrison-Halsted site and to the president development of a memorandum of agreement with the city on acquisition of the site. The full board accepted the site, and President Henry wrote Mayor Daley accordingly on February 17. In his letter Henry referred to the city's awareness of the problem of Hull-House and the continuation of its work, and he stated that the University would consider ways to memorialize the work of Jane Addams and Hull-House.[40]

One stage of the decision to locate the new campus had ended; the city and the University had agreed upon a site. "Mayor Daley was committed to Harrison-Halsted hook, line and sinker, and [felt] that

[40]UICC Archives and Author's Papers: Board of Trustees, Committee on General Policy, report, February 15, 1961; and Henry to Daley, February 17, 1961. *Chicago Daily News,* February 10, 1961.

sometime during 1962 at least something of a symbolic nature had to take place (such as turning the first shovel of earth) by way of evidencing to the public that the die was irrevocably cast. . . . [He] would do everything humanly possible to enable the trustees to keep their target date [of September 1964 for opening the Chicago campus]."[41] But, despite this commitment, the opposition of residents of the Harrison-Halsted area who would be displaced led to an unplanned delay.

[41]Memorandum of conversation, July 13, 1962, "Congress Circle Campus: Acquisition of Site," Legal Counsel's Office, UIUC.

CHAPTER 6
The Community Responds

. . . when you have a good neighborhood, you have a good city.

Richard J. Daley (one of his last public remarks,
December 20, 1976), quoted in Eugene Kennedy,
Himself! The Life and Times of Richard J. Daley (New
York: Viking Press, 1978), p. 8.

THE AREA offered by the city and accepted
by the University in February 1961 was among the oldest areas with
one of the most colorful histories in the city. (See Map 2.)

In 1856, when Charles Hull built the structure that became known
as Hull-House at Halsted and Polk streets, the area was a half-rural,
market-garden district on the outskirts of the city. It later became a
fashionable area, with many large mansions lying between Harrison
on the south and the Haymarket on the north. But by 1871, when the
Great Chicago Fire began near that spot, the area had already become
a crowded community; and after 1871 it became an entry point into
the city for waves of European immigrants.

In 1889, when Jane Addams asked city officials for the most
crowded area in the city, she was told to go to Halsted and Blue
Island. By that time the native American populace had given way to
successive overlapping waves of Germans, Irish, Scandinavians, and
later Bohemians, Russians, East European Jews, Greek, and Italians.

[By] the turn of the century more than 20 different immigrant groups
resided in the area. The major elements included Eastern European
Jews, Bohemians, Italians (who constituted the largest single group
after about 1910), and Irish (who controlled ward politics, although
after the 1890s they were in the minority).

In 1884, a total of only 279 Italian immigrants lived in the large
expanse stretching west of the Chicago River to Ashland between Van
Buren and Twelfth Streets. Just 14 years later the number [in the Near
West Side Colony] had grown to more than 4,000. . . . In 1898 the
district [of Italian population] was located between the River and
Halsted Street. . . . This area contained some of the worst housing in
the city and residents . . . moved at the first opportunity they had.
Thus by 1920 the Italian population in the blocks between Halsted and
Ashland had greatly increased while the older community to the east

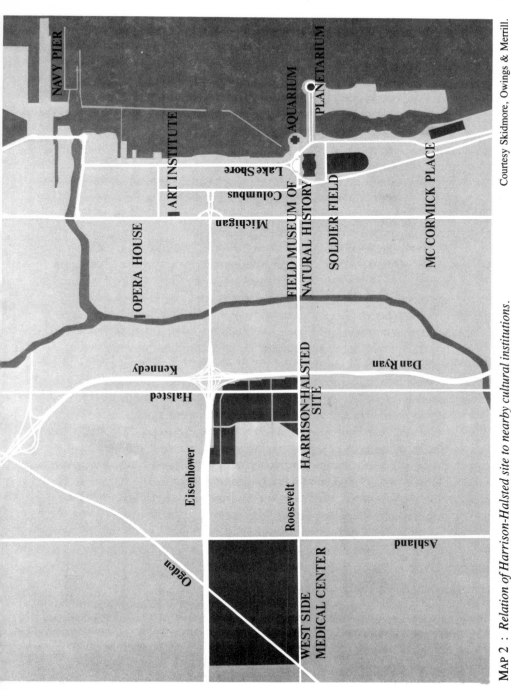

MAP 2 : *Relation of Harrison-Halsted site to nearby cultural institutions.*

had declined drastically. In subsequent years, the center of Italian population continued to shift westward . . . but the blocks between Halsted and Ashland continued to hold many in the neighborhood.[1]

In 1899 the first Italian Roman Catholic church in the neighborhood, the Holy Guardian Angel Church, was built. By 1911 the parish was divided and a second church, Our Lady of Pompeii, was constructed to serve the large number of Italians in the area west of Morgan Street. Most of the immigrants were from southern Italy, and they had been attracted to the area by the presence of other Italians already there and by low rents. They worked mainly as unskilled laborers at first. They sought to live cheaply, to save, and to educate their children. When they had saved enough, they either bought property in the area or moved farther west. By the 1930s, Edith Abbott points out, many of their children had moved from the old neighborhood to the west; and, as immigration was reduced, the population of Italian birth or descent remaining in the old area of settlement was also reduced. Nelli points out in his book that in the heart of the Italian area, bounded by Van Buren and Roosevelt, Morgan and Racine, the population fell from 15,700 in 1910 to 8,500 in 1930; about three-fourths of the latter population was Italian.

From the turn of the century onwards, Greek immigrants also moved into the area in large numbers; but their numbers were far lower than the Italians. In 1894 fewer than one hundred Greeks lived in the Hull-House ward; by 1908 that number had risen to five hundred; and by 1914 it had reached two thousand. The Greeks settled in the area of the intersection of Blue Island and Halsted; and they established many stores, coffee shops, and other businesses along both Blue Island and Halsted south of Harrison.[2] Many Greeks also moved west as their incomes rose and their children became more educated. When immigration stopped in the mid-1920s, the

---

[1]For a history of Italians in this area, see Humbert S. Nelli, *The Italians in Chicago, 1880–1930* (New York: Oxford University Press, 1970), especially ch. 2, "Patterns of Settlement," and pp. 204–6; for the summary quotation, see his short article, "Chicago's Near West Side Italian Community in the 1960s," *Identity* (April 1977), p. 51.

[2]See Edith Abbott, *Tenements of Chicago, 1908–1935* (Chicago: University of Chicago Press), pp. 93–97, 97–98; see also Jordan Levin, "Our Lady of Pompeii Parish," and "A History of Holy Trinity Greek Orthodox Church and Socrates School," two short histories prepared in 1963 when he was consulting historian for the Department of Urban Renewal.

number of Greeks actually residing in the area declined, with many of these older people; but the Greek businesses remained.

Even though immigration from southern Europe had largely ended by 1930, movement into this convenient, low-rent area did not stop. During the 1940s and afterward, large numbers of blacks, Mexicans, and Puerto Ricans were attracted to the area, while redevelopment in the form of public housing and new highways was forcing some of the older residents to move out. (The public housing of the 1930s was not built for blacks, however; it was meant for low-income whites and was at first occupied by them.)

In the next chapter, where I deal with the effect of the campus upon the neighborhood, I will present detailed data on the changing character of the neighborhood population from 1950 on. One consequence of the thinning of the Italian and Greek population in this area was that the number of people per housing unit fell substantially. "By 1960 . . . four room apartments which a half century before had accomodated 15 to 30 people typically housed three or four, and sometimes only one or two."[3]

By the late 1950s the Italians lived mainly in the area bounded on the east and west by Halsted and Ashland and on the north and south by Harrison and Roosevelt, with the exception of the Jane Addams project and the area of the Holy Family–St. Ignatius complex. The Greeks who remained were along Blue Island and Halsted. By then blacks had largely displaced whites in the public housing units along Roosevelt Road. Public housing units along and to the north of Taylor were still largely occupied by whites, but blacks had begun to move into them. Blacks also lived along Blue Island in significant numbers, and some single black families lived throughout the area. Although Mexicans were scattered throughout the area, those blocks near the mainly Mexican church of St. Francis Assisi on Roosevelt Road had more Mexican than Italian families. Puerto Rican families lived mainly on the western and northern peripheries of the area along Ashland Avenue and Harrison Street, with a few living on the adjacent side streets.[4]

[3]Nelli, *Identity*, p. 53.

[4]Florence Scala, written comments on early draft of this study, February 1978, Author's Papers; see also Gerald D. Suttles, *Social Order of the Slum* (Chicago: University of Chicago Press, 1968), pp. 15–20.

But while the number of Italians in the near West Side area had declined from 1920 to 1960, political power had shifted toward the Italians. In the period before the mid-1920s the predominatly Italian 19th Ward was dominated by an Irish organization headed by the notorious Johnny Powers, who beat off both the reform challenges led by Jane Addams early in the century and the Italian challenges led by Anthony D'Andrea in the violent 1921 election. But although Powers won the election and D'Andrea was killed soon afterward and although Powers succeeded in gerrymandering the large 19th Ward into a group of smaller wards in each of which the Italians were a minority, by the end of the 1920s Italians from that area had won control over the district, having been elected to the City Council and other positions. Initially political power shifted to gang leaders like Jim Colosimo, Johnny Torrio, and Al Capone, who wanted protection. Capone, although ostensibly a Republican, supported any local politicians and organizations that would not interfere with his gang activities.[5] The role of the gangs both in Italian politics and in the Republican party in the city has diminished since Thompson's mayoralty in the 1920s.

As a result of the Great Depression and the popularity of Franklin D. Roosevelt, many Italians switched to the Democratic party, and Italian political leaders from the area became part of the city's Democratic organization. While few Italian leaders have been elected to city- or state-wide office, Italian leaders from this and nearby districts have been elected regularly to the City Council, the state legislature, and Congress; and some, such as Alderman Vito Marzullo, exercise power in the city-wide organization beyond their wards. The Italian representatives in the state legislature have also exercised more influence as a group than as individuals, through the informal organization of a West Side Bloc. That bloc has included Italian legislators from both parties who have acted together for the interests of their districts, at times crossing party lines in a fashion that is somewhat unpredictable even to party leaders. When Vito Marzullo was in the state legislature, he introduced the Medical Center Bill in 1941, establishing the center district in the near West Side, and legislators from the area since that time have always had an

[5]On this, see Nelli, *Italians in Chicago,* chs. 5 and 7.

interest in the University. (In the early 1950s Senator Libonati played an important role in the controversy over Krebiozen that involved Dean Ivy of the Medical Center and contributed to the resignation of President Stoddard.) At the time of the decision to offer the Harrison-Halsted area to the University, John D'Arco was the dominant political figure and alderman from what had by then become the 1st Ward. While he apparently was informed of the city's intention before the offer was made, the decision was made over his head; and, as we have seen, he had little choice but to go along with it. This was in spite of the strong party organization in his ward and the many city employees living in that ward.

Another significant force in the area was Hull-House, even though it had abandoned district politics after Jane Addams's effort to defeat Johnny Powers had failed. Its political influence was indirect, through the prestige and influence of Jane Addams and others at government levels above the ward. But it played a very significant social and educational role in the district, not only assisting Italian immigrants to become acclimated to American conditions and dealing with physical and social problems in the immediate area, but also educating the children and grandchildren of the immigrants.

Florence Scala has an eloquent tribute to Hull-House in her conversations with Studs Terkel:

> I grew up around Hull-House. . . . My father was a tailor, and we were just getting along in a very poor neighborhood. He never had money to send us to school; but we were not impoverished. When one of the teachers suggested that our mother send us to Hull-House, life began to open up. At the time, the neighborhood was dominated by gangsters and hoodlums. They were men from the old country, who lorded it over the people in the area. It was the day of moonshine. The influence of Hull-House saved the neighborhood. It never really purified it. . . . I don't think Hull-House intended to do that. But it gave us . . . well, for the first time my mother left that darn old shop to attend Mother's Club once a week. . . . Hull-House gave you a little insight into another world. There was something else to life besides sewing and pressing.[6]

Ernest Giovangelo, her brother, also remembers his Hull-House

[6]Studs Terkel, *Division Street: America* (New York: Avon, 1968), pp. 29–30.

experiences as among the profoundest of his life; even though a boy, he was selected to be one of the pallbearers from the neighborhood at Jane Addams's funeral. In the 1920s and 30s, some of the young people in the neighborhood especially found a center for activity and hope at Hull-House; although others—old and young—considered it an outside organization to be dealt with warily both because it was run by non-Italians and outsiders and because it was disruptive of older patterns.

The 1930s was a period of depression and decline in the area, and some changes were forced upon it. The Jane Addams public-housing project was built without first consulting the people who lived in the district. Older inhabitants were forced out in what seemed an arbitrary fashion, and newer ones moved in. The manner of deciding on this project created resentment among area residents; and while matters remained quiet during the war, some of the younger returning soldiers were determined to take active steps to revive the neighborhood and retain control over what happened in it.

The nucleus of an organization of Italian residents and returning veterans already existed in the West Side Community Committee. In part stimulated by the likelihood of new building projects in the area and in part by state legislation passed in 1947 to deal with blighted areas, these community members met with Hull-House director Russell Ballard late that year and in early 1948 to explore what the community might do to take advantage of the new opportunities and to prevent undesirable changes. Ballard, who had been appointed director of Hull-House in 1943, felt himself still somewhat an outsider in the district. He believed that Hull-House should support neighborhood efforts both for their own sake and also to strengthen ties with the young, native-born generation in the community.[7]

It is not my intention here to write a history of community planning in the Hull-House area from 1947 to 1960. That history was a complex one, involving many people and organizations, some of the organizations already existing and some set up later for special purposes. While it is not necessary for this study to know the details

[7]For the history of these efforts during the late 1930s, the postwar period, the origins of the West Side Community Committee, and relations with Hull-House, see Anthony Sorrentino, *Organizing against Crime* (New York: Human Sciences Press, 1977), pp. 90–95, 174, 205–9. Sorrentino was a leader in these community efforts.

of that history, an understanding of the aims behind the community planning efforts, its successes and failures, and of the relationship between various elements within the community and each other, as well as with the city and Hull-House, will make it possible to better understand why the mayor could successfully offer the Harrison-Halsted site to the University in 1960 and why the community responded as it did—with strong but belated opposition.

Before beginning a review of the community planning for this area after World War II, mention should be made of the place of this area in a famous earlier plan. The Burnham Plan of Chicago in 1909 had a prominent place for the near West Side:

> Congress Street was to be turned into a broad boulevard leading to an impressive Civic Center. . . . The new City Hall sat in the center of a pentagonal public square that was surrounded on four sides by governmental buildings. This new center, located just southwest of the Loop, was designed to instill life into a dying neighborhood as well as to remove a major cause of downtown congestion.

In addition to turning Congress Street into a boulevard, the plan envisaged widening of Twelfth Street (Roosevelt Road) into a boulevard.

The proposed plan is shown in Map 3. What is perhaps most significant is that the location originally planned for the Civic Center Plaza became the Chicago Circle, the center of the city's expressway system. The idea of a Civic Center there, now replaced by the junction of the city's expressways, may have contributed to both the idea of the city's planners of placing a campus adjacent to the Chicago Circle in what the plan considered a dying neighborhood and the acceptability of that idea to the city's establishment.[8]

A Temporary Organizing Committee of residents of the district was set up in 1947. This committee met, had frequent discussions concerning the district's problems, and decided that a planning board would be necessary as the vehicle for developing a plan. Hull-House financed this early stage and was responsible for the key person in the

[8]Perry Duis, *Chicago: Creating New Traditions* (Chicago: Chicago Historical Society, 1976), pp. 52, 54; Daniel H. Burnham and Edward H. Bennett, *Plan of Chicago*, intro. Wilbert R. Hasbrouck (reprint ed., New York: DaCapo Press, 1970), facing p. 100.

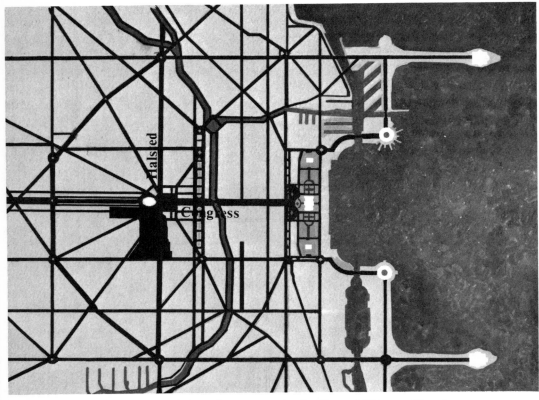

MAP 3 : *Proposed City Center area in the Plan of Chicago (Burnham Plan), 1909.* Note the "Chicago Circle, major focus of the city's expressway system . . . as the civic center plaza" at the intersection of Halsted and Congress streets.
Source: H. M. Mayer and R. C. Wade, *Chicago: Growth of a Metropolis* (Chicago: University of Chicago Press, 1969), p. 277.

effort. He was Eri Hulbert, Jane Addams's nephew, who was hired as consultant to the committee in August 1948.

Hulbert was born, and had lived, near Hull-House for many years. He knew the people in the area and had the confidence of many of the residents as well as of the Hull-House board and the city establishment. He also knew many figures of national stature and had a wide range of experience in the field of housing. Perhaps most important, he has been described as a man with a vision and a genius for articulating that vision and getting people to work with him toward it. The vision was set forth to the Temporary Organizing Committee in his own words shortly after he began his work:

> No community in the nation has ever created a practical vision of its future that has grown from the people with participation by every kind of person, group and interest. The people of the Near West Side . . . can be the first to demonstrate in this field that democracy can function practically, economically and intelligently in remaking the world they live in. There is a new community possible for people with real pride in the place in which they live, work and play.[9]

Attached to Hulbert's vision was a hard-headed awareness of how things get done in Chicago. Before accepting the offer, he

> . . . discussed the question with the Chicago Plan Commission, the Housing Coordinator's Office, the Land Clearance Commission, the Chicago Housing Authority, the Metropolitan Housing and Planning Council . . . and still others. Without exception they agreed that a local planning effort . . . was not a duplication of the efforts of others. . . . Without exception they agreed that they, as city-wide agencies, were responsible only for special phases of building and that only on the local level could all interests be considered together. . . . [Numerous] officials are sympathetic to the idea of a planning board in our area.[10]

And, finally, Eri Hulbert saw the success of this as a message to the whole country. He said repeatedly, "If conservation can't work in

[9]Ernest Giovangelo to Russell Ballard, February 25, 1957, "Final Report (September 1952 through October 1956) on the Near West Side Planning Board Administration of Wieboldt Grant . . . ," p. 1. Scala Papers.

[10]Eri Hulbert, quoted in P. B. Johnson, "Citizen Participation in Urban Renewal," mimeographed (Chicago: Hull-House Association, 1960), p. 29.

Hyde Park it can't work anywhere, but if conservation *can* work on the Near West Side, it can work anywhere."[11]

An early issue was over the preparation and timing of a plan. Various groups pressed the Temporary Organizing Committee to rapidly prepare such a detailed plan for the community. The advocates of this approach did not realize that such a hastily prepared plan would not properly represent the needs and ideas of the whole community. Hulbert, by persistent educational efforts, was eventually able to persuade the people of the area that a successful plan must be prepared through a process that would involve the whole community in discussion, argument, and exchange; it was not to be a document handed down from on high. The originally small committee was gradually broadened to include wide-ranging, representative elements from the community; and on June 15, 1949, at a public meeting attended by over 500 residents of the area, the committee was converted into a permanent organization, the Near West Side Planning Board (NWPB), with its function to represent the entire community in the preparation and implementation of plans for renewal of the near West Side area. By planning was meant not a single plan of slum clearance, but a combination of "a variety of approaches [including] . . . new housing, conservation of good housing, . . . new zoning and other means combined in a single area."[12]

The June 15 meeting was only a start of the struggle for community support and involvement. There were many problems. One of the most persistent and also one that all were aware of was the need for a representative community mix both in terms of activity and ethnicity. Of 340 members of the Near West Side Planning Board in 1950, 235 were local residents, 50 were business firms, and 55 were from out of the area. Of the ethnic mixture in this group, the Italians had the largest representation, with 128 members, the Blacks 70, Mexicans 15, the Greeks only 5, and 122 from other groups. There were also problems in the relationship between this new organization and the existing centers of power, the Catholic Church and the alderman and his political organization. Probably the most nagging and long-

[11]Giovangelo to Ballard, "Final Report . . . on . . . Administration of Wieboldt Grant," p. 4, emphasis added.

[12]Ibid., p. 2. Information in the early part of this paragraph was given me by Ernest Giovangelo (interviews October 26, November 16, 1977, Author's Papers).

standing problem was the money—there was never enough money to do what was needed, and there was a constant need to appeal for funds beyond the dues paid by residential contributions, to Hull-House, to various foundations, and to the staff itself in the form of payless days.

The difficulty of achieving an ethnic mix is shown by the small Greek and Mexican membership. In part the difficulty before 1955 arose from lack of funds to make a major effort in those communities, while the Italian community's support was the basis for starting and continuing the effort. Subsequently businessmen from both of these ethnic groups cooperated actively with the Hull-House Community Participation program in seeking ways to continue their businesses in the Harrison-Halsted Redevelopment Project or to participate in a proposed international shopping center.

The confrontation with the existing powers in the community occurred early and then ended. Father Barton of the local Catholic Church was sharply critical of the early work of the Temporary Organizing Committee, but other priests in the area supported it, and gradually "opposition by any church disappeared from the record."[13]

A potentially greater threat took the form of a conflict that opposed the Near West Side Planning Board against the alderman and the area's dominant political powers. If that conflict had led to a split between the West Side Community Committee, which represented many of the Italian residents, and the Planning Board, it might have proved disastrous for the latter, but it did not.

The initial form taken by this conflict was a clash over an ordinance introduced in January 1950 by Alderman Pistilli of the 1st Ward before the Chicago Plan Commission and ultimately before the City Council.[14] This ordinance arose from a fear within the neighborhood that it would be arbitrarily cleared. On January 20 Alderman Pistilli, through an intermediary, took the lead in introducing an ordinance to "deblight" the area bounded by Harrison Street, Roosevelt Road, Halsted Street, and Ashland Avenue, with the recommendation that it

---

[13]Johnson, "Citizen Participation in Urban Renewal," p. 42. For data on ethnic composition of NWPB in 1950, see "Summary Outline of Citizen Participation in Urban Renewal Planning . . . for the Chicago Near West Side Community with Special Reference to Harrison-Halsted and Adjacent Areas," n.d., p. 53. Scala Papers.

[14]Johnson, "Citizen Participation in Urban Renewal," ch. 4, describes this incident.

be "reclassified with certain exceptions as *a proper area for rehabilitation of existing structures.*"

The Near West Side Planning Board made its objections to the ordinance known privately rather than publicly. It expressed the position that the measure, called the Pistilli Ordinance, had been formulated arbitrarily. It was not based on facts, it bypassed usual procedures of designating areas, it was loose in its wording, and it would not make it possible to work with the Land Clearance Commission in the area. The Planning Board further objected because the whole thing had been done in the old way of doing things in Chicago.

Tensions were high on the issue, which was considered to be a test of loyalty to Hull-House or to the community; and some members of the community who opposed the original version of the proposed ordinance were considered turncoats.

Lengthy discussions were held on the matter. Both sides, recognizing the genuine fears on the part of the community, desired to reach a compromise; and the Planning Board did some research on housing in the area. A revised Pistilli Ordinance was passed in May 1950. It declared most of the district a conservation area, but it excepted from that designation approximately 45 acres. That excepted area subsequently became the basis for the Harrison-Halsted project, since it was declared suitable for clearance and initial redevelopment. In part this was a victory for the Planning Board, which had forced recognition of itself as central to the carrying out of research on a planning matter before a decision was made; but it also indicated lines of possible future tension between the Planning Board and the community's political powers. It was also strong evidence, at an early date, of the active support of all parts of the community for efforts for its preservation and improvement, of its fear of large-scale forced clearance, and of its willingness to take measures to protect itself against such action.

Probably the most serious continuous problem of the Planning Board in this period was lack of money. Contributions from individuals and firms never met the budget, and additional funds were always being sought. Some of this might have been eased if the board had compromised its aims. At least one leading land company in the Loop offered the board a large amount of money if it would agree to plan for clearance of much of the area, but this offer was rejected.

Hull-House provided minimal base funding. Some additional funding during the early period came from the Field and Wieboldt Foundations; and early in 1955, as a result of Eri Hulbert's efforts, Hull-House received a $41,000 grant from the Schwartzhaupt Foundation for a community participation project in the area. This provided long-term funds through Hull-House, but the funds were to be channeled to the Planning Board. In addition, an arrangement was worked out with the West Central Association (WCA) for the Planning Board to provide paid consultation service for that organization, which represented the large business firms north of Congress and west of the Loop. It was hoped that this would provide long-term business support in funding the NWPB. In fact, it did revive the WCA, but it led to a flow of income and human resources *from* the Planning Board *to* the WCA rather than the reverse.[15]

In spite of these problems, the Planning Board had an impact on planning for the area. For example, in 1951 it worked with the Chicago Plan Commission and the Land Clearance Commission in the efforts of those city agencies to designate a 55-acre tract east of Halsted for clearance for industrial use. This was the first industrial relocation project in the country, and it was associated with a proposed residential project west of Halsted, which would serve to absorb many of the residents displaced by the proposed industrial project.[16]

Much of this progress came to a halt with Eri Hulbert's suicide in May 1955. The main link between Hull-House and the West Side community was broken by his death. The executive committee of the Near West Side Planning Board strongly favored the appointment of Ernest Giovangelo, the board's community relations technician, to serve as Hulbert's successor as board director, but Hull-House objected to his appointment. Hull-House immediately took the step of diverting the Schwartzhaupt grant, of which it had been the formal recipient, to a new Community Participation Project directly responsible to it and separate from the NWPB, rather than combined with it.

[15]Ibid., p. 146.

[16]Apart from the lengthy Johnson report (ibid.) and the short Giovangelo "Final Report . . . on . . . Administration of Wieboldt Grant," Sorrentino, *Organizing against Crime,* ch. 8, especially pp. 210–23, is the only published description of this effort. D. E. Mackelman, then commissioner of the city's Community Conservation Board, has thrown further light on this project by pointing out the role of city agencies (interview, March 10, 1978, Author's Papers).

Since the events following Hulbert's death were so vital to the future of the neighborhood, it is worth considering the response of Hull-House to that event. Although Giovangelo was the senior remaining person on the board's staff, Hull-House refused to accept him as either acting director or director of the Planning Board. The ostensible reason given, at a time when few people had training in urban planning, was that he did not have formal training in urban planning. At least several knowledgeable people still feel this was correct. Many of the Italian residents of the area, however, felt that the real reason was that Giovangelo was Italian and from the community. Hull-House officials were also afraid that the dominant political organization in the area would take over the Planning Board if Giovangelo was appointed director, even though he had been brought up at Hull-House, had been profoundly influenced by it, and he and his sister, Florence Scala, had shown their willingness to resist local political pressures by supporting Hulbert in the argument over the Pistilli Ordinance. The Hull-House officials were interested in redevelopment of the neighborhood, but they were reluctant to become involved with the local political figures whose support was essential for any action by the city government unless it was on their own terms. This position was opposite that of residents of the neighborhood, who felt Hull-House could not be trusted; Hull-House did not trust the neighborhood leadership either. In the past Hull-House, with its prestige, could bypass local political figures; but it could not do that on a major community redevelopment project.

After the death of Jane Addams, the Hull-House Board of Trustees had changed from a board that relied on her, simply accepting her needs, in effect serving as a vehicle through which one family financed her efforts. By the mid-1950s no single family could afford to meet its deficits, and the board was broadened to include business and political luminaries to provide funds. These had little interest in the neighborhood as such, especially as the need for such a community institution lessened as native-born Italians became successful. The new board saw Hull-House in a city-wide framework, as an organization to be run efficiently and "pay its way." Many of the new members had little real knowledge of the local community and believed the folklore that surrounded it. They were reluctant to entrust a vital project or a grant to an administrator from that community.

Near West Side scene (1940s) with Loop buildings in background.

Holy Guardian Angel parish building (church, school, and convent), the anchor of the Harrison-Halsted community, ready for occupancy in early 1959 and demolished in the early 1960s. Photo from *Humilitas, 75th Anniversary* (Melrose Park, Ill.: Missionary Fathers of St. Charles, n.d.).

The Harrison-Halsted business district looking north on Halsted from De Koven circa 1963. JANE ADDAMS MEMORIAL COLLECTION, LIBRARY, UICC.

Circle Campus viewed from the same vantage point in 1980.
FRANK O. WILLIAMS PHOTOGRAPH.

The Near West Side Planning Board meets in the residents' dining hall of Hull-House (circa 1950s). JANE ADDAMS MEMORIAL COLLECTION, LIBRARY, UICC.

Near West Side area women begin their battle to save the neighborhood (April 1961). *Chicago Sun-Times*.

University of Illinois students congratulate Mayor Daley on the Harrison-Halsted site decision (April 1961). *Chicago Sun-Times*.

After the Wieboldt grant ran out in 1956 and Hull-House diverted the Schwartzhaupt fund from the Near West Side Planning Board, the board gradually ended its work; it ceased to function by the latter half of 1957.[17] But during the eighteen-month interim period, the board succeeded in getting passed by the City Council three ordinances designating certain parts of the area for urban renewal. To do this, the board and its acting director, Ernest Giovangelo, worked with the alderman and ward committeeman, by then John D'Arco, to convince him of the desirability of the ordinances and to persuade him that he should introduce them, since his advocacy was essential to pass the ordinances. The three ordinances were the legal basis for the future redevelopment of the area.

In May 1956 the City Council approved the area bounded by the Congress Expressway on the north, the Chicago Public Housing projects on the south, the Harrison-Halsted project on the east and Ashland Boulevard on the west, as a conservation renewal area; and this was subsequently accepted by the federal government. In October of the same year, the City Council approved the designation of the Harrison-Halsted area as a "slum and blight" area for clearance and redevelopment; and this was subsequently approved by the state Housing Board.[18] But these very successes of the planning board, necessarily achieved by working with the alderman, helped convince Hull-House that Giovangelo had been captured by the local political organization; and while formal relationships were maintained, Hull-House continued the separation of its work and funds from the Planning Board.

Meanwhile, the Italian residents and businessmen in the area, working with Giovangelo and Alderman D'Arco, began their own development efforts. In early 1958 they hired Tibor Haring, an architect and city planner, to develop a proposed land-use plan to present to the Land Clearance Commission and to interested develop-

[17]For what follows I have relied heavily on conversations with Ernest Giovangelo (interviews October 26 and November 16, 1977, Author's Papers) and Florence Scala (interviews October 18 and December 5, 1977, ibid.), on files of the NWPB (Scala Papers), and on texts of City Council ordinances.

[18]The City Council also approved a third ordinance proposed by the NWPB, to create within the near West Side area the Blue Island–Thirteenth Street Shopping Center, which was to be developed by a local druggist, Nathan Roskin. This project, the first shopping center in a public-housing area, is actually to the south of the University area and neighborhood as defined for this study.

ers. This group of residents and businessmen also set up an association, the Harrison-Halsted Residents' and Businessmen's Association, to invest funds already received or to be received from the
condemnation of their property in the Harrison-Halsted area into new
homes or businesses in the same area; and they were prepared to put a
deposit on desired plots of land in exchange for conveyance. Several
outside developers were consulted, several of whom expressed serious interest, although none had committed himself at the time.

The Community Participation Project of Hull-House,[19] which was
financed by the Schwartzhaupt grant when Hull-House broke with the
Planning Board, had also begun to function and had established
relations with Greek and Mexican businessmen in the area adjacent to
Hull-House. These businessmen wished to continue their businesses
in the Harrison-Halsted project area, and they had expressed both an
interest and a willingness to invest funds in an international shopping
center in the area.

Apart from these developments by the local residents and businessmen, Hull-House itself was considering whether to sponsor a cooperative housing project of duplexes or three-story walkups for the area.
Although some anxiety was expressed in the Board of Trustees'
meetings concerning competition between this possible project and
the housing plans being considered by the association of Italian
residents, the Hull-House board requested of Real Estate Research
Corporation a study of the feasibility of such a cooperative housing
project, which study it discussed with Phil Doyle in early 1959.[20]

On the governmental level, in early 1958 the Land Clearance
Commission, the City Council, and the state Housing Board
approved a formal redevelopment plan for the 55.8 acre Harrison-
Halsted area for residential use. This designated purpose was also
formalized in the Central Area Plan of 1958. Contracts were entered
with the federal government to use federal funds to implement the
project, which would call for the purchase and clearance of more than
300 parcels of land and the relocation of more than 600 families. By
1960 the Commission had spent $6.9 million for land acquisition and

[19]Johnson, "Citizen Participation in Urban Renewal," chs. 12–15.

[20]Hull-House Board of Trustees, *Minutes*: February 28, 1958; April 24, 1959; and other
meetings in 1959. Scala Papers.

demolition of buildings. (Of this amount the city had contributed one-third and the federal government two-thirds under the provisions of the Urban Renewal Act). But clearance and demolition were spotty; only about half of the area had been acquired and cleared by 1960, and many families continued to live there.[21] (For an aerial photo of the area as of 1960, see illustration section.)

One major institution had entered the area, the Holy Guardian Angel School, which had been forced to relocate when the original school was demolished in the building of the South Expressway. In 1958 the church had spent about $600,000, collected in part from its parishioners, to construct a new school on Blue Island between Polk and Cabrini streets in the center of the area, and it intended eventually to build a permanent church there also. Although the school was the only project to come to fruition by late 1959, residents and business-men in the area, as well as Hull-House, were actively planning for future development; and the activities and plans of the various groups were known to city officials who had been in attendance at area meetings. In 1959 the mayor himself had attended the dedication of the Holy Guardian Angel School and had spoken warmly of it and of the project's future.

In 1960 most plans for the area were still possibilities and not actualities. The gap in activities between 1956, following Eri Hul-bert's death and passage of the area-development ordinances in the City Council, and 1958, when the effort for the area's redevelopment once again began in earnest, had what became the unfortunate con-sequence of leaving a large area controlled by the city close to the Loop and in large part empty, available for a campus for the Universi-ty of Illinois when no other site had been found. While residents in the area were optimistic about the future, many city officials were less so. They were skeptical of the success of the residents' efforts, of the neighborhood character of the area, and of the area's future. The popular reputation of the area, expressed in Burnham's plan as early as 1910 and in Havens's comments when he heard of the area as a possible site, was that it was one of the worst areas in the city. The

[21] Some residents feel today that this spotty clearance and demolition may have discouraged potential developers, who would have found it hard to put together a large enough block of land for development.

mayor's urgent need to find a site for the proposed campus, combined
with the opinion of city officials that the only way to reverse the
deterioration of the area and stablize it was by introducing a large
institution such as the University campus into it, led to the city's
decision in 1960 to offer the site to the University.

The neighborhood's sources of information concerning the city's
plans for the area were very weak: relations with Hull-House were
tenous, and the signals received through Alderman D'Arco were
weak and confusing. Thus the mayor's offer of the site to the University in September 1960 drew only a muted initial response from the
residents. The leaders of the neighborhood seemed to accept it without enthusiasm as inevitable, Hull-House was quiet, and the residents
showed little open reaction. But this calm was somewhat misleading;
a storm broke in February 1961 *after* the University accepted the site.
The outburst was not entirely unexpected by either Mayor Daley or
President Henry, although the character of the outburst and its
strength among the affected residents was greater than either had
anticipated.

The immediate events that occurred in early February as they
affected Hull-House are described in the minutes of the Board of
Trustees of Hull-House for that period.[22] On February 8, 1961,
James Downs declined to attend a special meeting of the board
because he had been involved in the city's decision. At this meeting
two motions were presented by the special committee of the board set
up to prepare a Hull-House position on the use of the Harrison-
Halsted site by the University. One motion favored use of the site for
that purpose on grounds that it would be an outstanding site for the
University and such use was to be preferred to the proposed residential use. The alternate motion opposed this use, pointing out Hull-
House's long involvement in the area and in plans for its redevelopment; it argued that the offering of this area to the University had been
done undemocratically. "No public hearings were scheduled, and
without the vehicle of a planning board, which is no longer in
existence, communication between the people and the decision mak-
ers has broken down. . . . To keep faith with our neighbors . . . the
Trustees . . . have no alternative but to officially oppose [this]."

---

[22]See Hull-House Board of Trustees, *Minutes,* February 8, 10, 13, 1961 (Scala Papers), on
these events and for quotations in this paragraph.

The Trustees met again on February 10, 1961, to vote on the two motions, James Downs again not attending. At that meeting a majority of 21 to 6, with 12 members abstaining, voted to oppose the proposal to locate the University of Illinois at the Harrison-Halsted site on grounds given in the second motion: no consultation with the neighborhood before making the proposal; no public hearings on the change in purpose of the project from residential use as called for in the ordinance creating the project to a university campus. After this vote James Downs felt he could not longer remain board president, although he remained on the board.

After this strong action the board retreated. On February 13 it adopted a motion taking no position on the location issue but insisting "that all proper public meetings be held prior to the making of this important decision." The board was split into many groups: those opposing the university location at Harrison-Halsted; those favoring that location; those worrying about what would happen to Hull-House itself at that location, some of whom felt the condemnation money would permit new efforts in other parts of the city; and those who felt some responsibility to the neighborhood with whose history Hull-House had been so deeply involved. The effect of this split was that the Hull-House board as a whole played a negligible role in the events that followed, except insofar as they dealt with the future of Hull-House itself. Some individuals on the board supported opposition to the mayor's decision, others supported the decision; but the board lacked strength as a united force on the location issue.

Since the board included some very influential members of the city and state's social, business, and political leadership, its unwillingness to sustain its February 10th opposition to location of the campus was a major blow to efforts within the neighborhood to block that location. The staff and several residents of Hull-House who were closely involved with the community by their work strongly supported the neighborhood opposition; but while this support was valuable, the position of the staff members carried little weight with the city's decision-makers. However, both the Hull-House trustees and staff were united on the need for a suitable memorial to Jane Addams and Hull-House at the original site. There was strong agitation at the local and national level, which included such figures as Eleanor Roosevelt, Senator Paul Douglas, Sidney Hillman's widow, members of the McCormick family, and others who supported such a memorial. The city and the University recognized this and changed the plans for the campus to retain and recreate the original Hull-House and dining quarters. With that, agitation on the part of Hull-House ended.

A more meaningful agitation was the spontaneous outburst of opposition from the residents of the area who would be displaced by the campus. This opposition influenced the relationship between the campus, the neighborhood, and the larger city of which it was a part. It was not an opposition led by local political leaders, who, while they generally opposed the decision, went along with what they saw to be a City Hall decision they could not fight. The incident that sparked the opposition was initiated by Father Scola, pastor of the Holy Guardian Angel Church, which would now be displaced a second time. He called a meeting in the parish hall on the night of February 13 to protest the decision. This meeting was attended largely by women of the area. The events that followed are recorded in a memorandum written shortly afterward by Ernest Giovangelo, who was on the staff of the Community Conservation Board, to Lew Hill, who was then assistant commissioner of the board, in response to questions from Hill concerning Giovangelo's involvement with the protest.[23]

Giovangelo's description of the events of the evening follows:

We [Florence Scala and himself] agreed that we would not participate beyond attending the meeting as interested residents.

At around 7:25 p.m. we arrived at the parish hall and found a jam-packed crowd, including reporters from all the daily newspspaers. About ten minutes after our arrival four residents came to Mrs. Scala and requested that she chair the meeting. Mrs. Scala indicated that she had no interest in chairing the meeting and only came . . . as a curious resident. Discussion by the four residents attempting to convince Mrs. Scala to chair the meeting went on for about fifteen minutes. Meanwhile the people in the hall began getting impatient and calling out. . . . Mrs. Scala then agreed to chair the meeting that night, and at the time, for that night only.

Mrs. Scala and I had no foreknowledge of the meeting or its purpose: to march on City Hall. . . . The reason Mrs. Scala was

---

[23]Ernest Giovangelo to Lew Hill, "Near West Side Citizens Protest Meeting against the University of Illinois Locating in the 'Harrison-Halsted' Area," February 27, 1961 (Scala Papers), pp. 1–2.

requested to chair the meeting by the residents was because they had known of her years of active participation on the Near West Side Planning Board and [that she] could intelligently chair the meeting and discuss the issues.

Of course, once Mrs. Scala accepted . . . she was "hooked." Newspaper accounts of the meeting reported Mrs. Scala as the leader. As a result, during the protest march about City Hall [on the next day] . . . reporters sought out Mrs. Scala. . . .

To indicate how unorganized and spontaneous this entire march was, neither Mrs. Scala nor any of the other women had given any thought to meeting with the Mayor. The suggestion came to Mrs. Scala from a reporter . . . [Georgie Anne Geyer, who] even arranged the meeting.

Due to the immense . . . [news] coverage given this event, and the follow-up stories . . . with Mrs. Scala, and the faith the many residents . . . have in [her], she emerged as the natural leader of the group.

A second public meeting was held at Hull-House on February 20. It was attended by over 500 people; and it, too, was chaired by Florence Scala. The local legislators must have been worried by the residents' reaction, because the district's representative to the state legislature also attended. He conveyed Alderman D'Arco's regrets that he could not attend, and he promised to fight against the action and quoted the alderman as saying the same. At this meeting various alternatives were presented to the protesters: to fight the decision in the City Council, to try to get the support of the Catholic Church, and to explore the legal alternatives. The assistant director of Hull-House, who also attended this meeting, described the prevailing attitude as follows: "The people are mad at Hull-House, at the alderman, at their representatives and at themselves."[24] Significantly, Father Scola participated in this meeting only in his personal capacity; he had been forbidden by the local church organization to participate as a representative of the Catholic Church. In the wider community, at about the same time, the Joint Action Committee and the business groups it represented gave up their efforts to locate the University at the Railroad Terminal site and pledged their support for the Harrison-Halsted site. Andrew Boemi, head of JAC, said that the West Side had been the group's second choice, and that one of his

[24]Ibid., p. 2; Hull-House Board of Trustees, *Minutes*, February 23, 1961, ibid.

group's major goals was to prevent location of the campus in Garfield Park.[25]

As a result of the February protest meetings and to serve as focus for the fight against the location decision, the Harrison-Halsted Community Group was formed, with Florence Scala at its head, to represent the residents who would be displaced by the decision. The executive committee of this group consisted mainly of housewives and a few men (both Italian and Mexican); several representatives of the Hull-House staff; and Jessie Binford, a close friend and associate of Jane Addams and the organizer and director of the Juvenile Protective Association, who was then retired and living at Hull-House. The group fought vigorously against the campus-location decision at every political forum available—before the Planning and Housing Committee of the City Council, before the City Council itself, before the University's Board of Trustees, before the Illinois Housing Board, in the State Legislature, and before the Federal Housing and Home Finance Agency.[26] It lost at every stage. However, President Henry, to calm fears of further expansion by the University to the west, wrote a letter on April 17, 1961, to Councilman Zelezinski, chairman of the Planning and Housing Committee of the City Council, stating "categorically that the University has no program for the enlargement of the [proposed site at Harrison and Halsted streets of about 106 acres]."[27] And the University thereafter felt it could not expand to the west.

Meanwhile, as predicted by Charles Havens when he first informed the University of the site, the city moved quickly to carry out all legal formalities, and at each stage the community group protested. By the end of March, the Land Clearance Commission had submitted a revision of the plan for the Harrison-Halsted project changing its use from residential to the campus. It also declared the adjoining Congress-Racine area, which had been part of the 240 acre "conservation area" approved in 1956, and the Roosevelt–Blue Is-

[25]*Chicago Tribune*, February 23, 1961.

[26]In hindsight the group may have erred in tactical terms by never favoring an alternate site, such as Garfield Park, in those public forums. As a result, it was considered to have only a negative reaction, and it did not tap support from other possible site areas.

[27]David Dodds Henry to A. V. Zelezinski, April 17, 1961, UICC Archives.

land area, for which no renewal action had been planned, to be "slum and blighted" areas under the meaning of the law, to be redeveloped largely as the site of the campus. In April the City Council Housing and Planning Committee approved those changes, and in May 1961 the City Council itself approved the amended project by passing the required ordinances. Hearings were held in June and July before the state Housing Board on the designation of the two new areas as redevelopment projects, and in August the board approved them. The next step was for the Federal Housing and Home Finance Agency to approve the change in plans for Harrison-Halsted and the plans for the two adjoining areas before the city could get federal funds for redevelopment of the area under the Urban Renewal Act. With this approval granted in March 1962, all administrative formalities were cleared.

Concurrently, necessary action was also being taken in the state legislature. A bill was passed in August 1961 amending previous state urban redevelopment legislation to specifically permit the city to convey land acquired for redevelopment to a public body having jurisdiction over schools (such as the University of Illinois) to use for building schools. It also permitted the city to set up a Department of Urban Renewal, which would combine the functions of the old Land Clearance Commission and Community Conservation Board. (John Duba, the mayor's assistant, was appointed to head that new department.) In June the legislature approved the budget of the University of Illinois, which included an appropriation of $4.6 million for the purchase of land for the proposed site. In the budget debate, an attempt made, under the leadership of Representative Granata from the Harrison-Halsted district, to delete that item was defeated.

With all efforts to overturn the location decision at the administrative and legislative level defeated, the Harrison-Halsted Community Group turned to the courts. It sought in both state and federal courts to overturn the decision on grounds that public hearings on the site's use were not in good faith, that declaration of the Congress-Racine and Roosevelt–Blue Island areas as "slum and blighted" areas was unwarranted, and that these actions were contrary to law. There followed a lengthy process of filing suits and appealing to the Illinois and U.S. Supreme Courts, which delayed the opening of the campus for more than a year. The arguments were repeatedly turned down in the courts, finally by the U.S. Supreme Court in May 1963. Even though lawyers for the group were most cooperative and helpful, the costs for a poor community were expensive. These costs could only be met by voluntary contributions from within the community, by outside well-wishers, and by the use of Jessie Binford's savings.

But, apart from its defeat in the courts, the community also lost because it had no political support from groups with "clout" in the city or country. The Hull-House board had clout, but it was split and took no stand on the issue. The opposition leaders had appealed to the Catholic Church, which might have been expected to offer support because of the large Catholic population in the area, but the church did not want "to seem to be trying to intrude on a political decision affecting public education."[28] Community leaders had then appealed to such leaders of the liberal establishment in the state as Senator Paul Douglas and Adlai Stevenson II but without success. They had appealed to Congressman Dawson, the political leader of the city's blacks, but he did not reply. They had asked Saul Alinsky for help, but he was busy with other activities in South Chicago and could not help. The newspapers, in their editorials, favored the location decision, not so much for the site itself as for bringing to an end an issue that had dragged on so long. Some columnists and reporters, e.g., Jack Mabley and Georgie Ann Geyer, supported the opposition; but they did not exert enough influence to make a difference. One important Republican political leader, Richard Ogilvie, supported the group; but his support did not have much effect on a Democratic mayor.

The small but very visible and vocal Harrison-Halsted Community Group consisted of about 300 women and their families. When several hundred of these women picketed City Hall and sat in the mayor's office, they were assured of media attention, public interest, and popular sympathy. They were embarrassing to the mayor, who knew how to deal with men but was uncomfortable in dealing with actively protesting women. Support for the group was strongest among those area residents whose homes and small businesses would

---

[28]"Testimony of Msgr. John Egan before the Chicago City Council Committee on Planning and Housing Concerning the Near West Side Urban Renewal Project," September 18, 1961. Author's Papers.

be cleared to make way for the campus. This support crossed over the usual ethnic and racial boundaries. Blacks, Mexicans, Puerto Ricans, and Greeks all worked closely with Florence Scala and the Italians in opposing the city and the University.[29] In addition, blacks and Mexicans from other sections of the city, who had earlier been displaced by the city's mass clearance programs, helped by picketing, raising funds, and attending public meetings.

But within the larger community bounded by Roosevelt and Congress, by Halsted and Ashland, support for the opposition was far weaker. In areas west of Morgan or Racine that were not scheduled for clearance, residents who had been somewhat reassured by President Henry's promise not to expand were sympathetic toward relatives and neighbors who were to be displaced, but they were not active supporters. The ward's leading Italian politicans felt they could not fight the decision; Alderman Marzullo in the neighboring district felt the same and supported the mayor, in part because he objected to the unorthodox methods of protest used by the women, whom he considered "a bunch of crazies." Many men living in the area worked for the city and owed their jobs to the local political organization; they were not willing to jeopardize those jobs by opposing the city (even though they may have sympathized with the residents who were being forced out and may have permitted their wives to support them). Although several of the younger Italian men, e.g., Oscar D'Angelo and Emil Peluso, supported the site decision because, for a variety of reasons, they felt location of the campus in the neighborhood would be good for the area, few took a positive public position. Leading business firms in the area, among them the Central National Bank, which had supported the planning effort, and John M. Smyth Furniture Company, which had been displaced earlier by the Expressway, felt they had little choice but to move elsewhere.

Apart from direct agitation and legal action against the decision, Florence Scala took the political step of running for alderman from the 1st Ward in the City Council elections of February 1963 as a write-in independent candidate. She lost the election but received

[29]One Spanish-speaking woman from the area told me of her father's having given the rent money he received one month to a fund-raiser for the protesting Harrison-Halsted group.

about one-third of the vote. Considering the power of the 1st Ward organization and that many families in the ward held jobs in the city government, she did not do too poorly; in fact, she was considered a sufficient threat to be offered a bribe to withdraw.[30] Her support within the ward probably reflected hard-core opposition to the campus that was not dependent upon the organization, since a vote for her would have involved a risk for those so voting.

Another political consequence that may have resulted from this protest and that was costly to the mayor in the short run was the 1962 defeat of a city bond issue for public improvements associated with urban renewal. While this bond issue was supported by newspapers and city banks, it was opposed by the Harrison-Halsted Community Group and its city-wide allies, including columnist Jack Mabley. This opposition apparently contributed heavily to the defeat of that bond issue, with the opposing voters asking, "Why should we pay for a 'harrison-halsted'?"[31]

Perhaps the most ironic comment on the entire opposition campaign was that the Near West Side Planning Board had once opposed the Pistilli Ordinance against clearing the area on the ground that it was offered without discussion or prior research. But the Pistilli Ordinance was in the normal way of things in Chicago. Now a second decision had been handed down from on high—this by Mayor Daley—and pioneering work and plans carefully laid over a period of almost fifteen years by area residents and the Near West Side Planning Board were wiped out. When that work had begun, its purpose was to show that a neighborhood could plan democratically for itself and thereby save itself; and if it could be done there, it could be done anywhere. The mayor's action had dashed that hope.

One legacy of the battle over the site was the poor relationship that existed between the campus and the neighborhood in the decade following the campus's opening in 1965. University planners had felt that one disadvantage of the site was its poor environment; and, to

[30]Interview with Florence Scala, October 18, 1977, Author's Papers. The bribe was offered in October 1962. In addition, one night, after a lengthy sit-in at the mayor's office, her home was bombed, apparently as a warning; but no injuries were sustained.

[31]Interview with Jack Mabley, March 8, 1978, Author's Papers. Georgie Anne Geyer, "The Heritage of Jane Addams: Florence Scala Fills the Void," *Chicago Scene* 5 (January 1964):27.

better control the campus and manage security within, a masonry wall was built between the campus and the community along the Morgan, Taylor, and Harrison street sides of the campus. With the racial unrest in the city during the 1960s, including the area just south of Roosevelt Road, some of the neighborhood residents feared and resented black students especially but also white and Asian students with lifestyles different from those of the old neighborhood. Some local youth gangs attacked students, but some area residents also intervened to rescue them.[32] Indicative of some of the feeling that still exists is the reference to the Circle Campus as "a huge fortress" in Anthony Sorrentino's recent and generally sympathetic book.[33] New faculty members certainly have heard rumors and stories of that feeling of suspicion; and popular books such as those by Mike Royko and Studs Terkel already cited, speak of the campus as an alien institution imposed upon the city and neighborhood by a dictatorial mayor. Even today, when representatives of the campus meet with local legislators, some faculty members feel an atmosphere of suspicion of the campus that may stem from the manner of its birth.[34] This issue of the effects of the campus will be examined more closely in the next chapter.

[32]Interview with Florence Scala, December 5, 1977, Author's Papers; Suttles, *Social Order of the Slum*, pp. 120–21.

[33]Sorrentino, *Organizing against Crime*, p. 225.

[34]David Dodds Henry stated that during the years of his presidency relations were good between the University and city legislators. Interview, December 2, 1977, Author's Papers.

CHAPTER 7

The Effects of the Location of the Campus upon the City, the Neighborhood, and the University

It is impossible to say that New York would have been a better city if Robert Moses had never lived. It is possible to say only that it would have been a different city.

Robert A. Caro, *The Power Broker* (New York: Vintage Books, 1975), p. 21.

THE MAIN REASONS for location of the campus at Harrison-Halsted were that all parties involved agreed that there should be a campus in the city and that the Harrison-Halsted site was the only chosen site upon which the city and University could agree within the constraints in which they operated. The choice was a compromise; it was no one's first, or even second, choice before 1959.

It is quite possible to argue that the benefit/cost ratio would have been higher at some other site, but no other appropriate site was in fact available within the time in which the decision had to be made. It is also possible to argue that it would have been preferable if no site had been chosen at that time and that more years should have been allowed to lapse rather than choose the Harrison-Halsted site. In that case it is doubtful whether the University of Illinois would have been in Chicago at all, and it is questionable whether another university would have replaced it. That would have been even more doubtful if it had taken as long to make a decision to locate another campus in the city as it ultimately took to make the decision to locate the new University of Illinois campus.

Thus, in looking at the results of the campus, the real comparison that has to be made is not between several hypothetical alternative sites, most of which were unavailable, but between the campus site chosen and no campus site or an alternative campus site with only a low probability of actual construction. When the search for a site was begun, it was possible to examine a variety of alternatives and to select the best one on the basis of acceptable criteria. But each time a preferred site was ruled out for one reason or another, the final choice narrowed, within the limits of the time and space constraints, to an all-or-nothing choice.

Some members of the Harrison-Halsted Community Group who strongly opposed location of the site in that area at the expense of their homes and business felt they may have made a strategic error in not proposing an alternate site; but, in fact, there probably was no real alternative they could have suggested *at that late date* with a reasonable chance of being fulfilled within the time limits. Both the mayor and the representative of the University knew that. It could be argued that a different mayor with a different set of political interests would have been able to look at all the alternatives at some earlier date and to offer a better site. That may be possible, but it is purely hypothetical and ignores the goals and real constraints within which the actual mayor functioned; and there is no reason to believe that another choice would have been better.

In looking at the effects of the campus upon the city and neighborhood in which it was placed, I will split the analysis into two parts: first the choice between a city as opposed to a suburban location; and, second, the choice between locating in one neighborhood in the city as compared with locating in another. A major goal of Mayor Daley in his negotiations with the University was to place the campus within the city of Chicago, preferably close to its center. He persuaded the University to accept this preference by his funding offer. In my opinion that was a correct decision. The effects of the campus would have been different if it had been located at Miller Meadows or at the Riverside Golf Club, although not if it had been located at the Railway Terminal, Garfield Park, or Northerly Island.

If the campus had a suburban location, I expect that both the number and character of students attending would have been significantly different. The difference in number would not have been noticeable initially. Between about 1965 and 1970 the demand for higher education was so great that the campus would have been fully occupied wherever it was located. But I believe the effect of the location on the number of students would have been felt after 1970, when the demand for higher education declined as the postwar baby boom came to an end.

Although it was understood that public transportation facilities would have been built if the campus had been located at either of the suburban locations, it is probable that a significantly smaller proportion of the potential student body would have traveled to such a campus by public transportation than to the Harrison-Halsted location. Instead, far more students would have had to have an automobile, either of their own or in the family.

Because of the suburban location and the distance, more of the students would have been expected to come, at least initially, from the suburbs; their families would probably have had a higher income than those of potential students from within the city. When the space for potential students was short, that would have had little effect on the total demand, since suburban students would not have had much choice of alternative colleges. But as the demand for higher education declined, it is likely that relatively more suburban students than city students would have chosen to go away from home to college, because they could afford to go and the space would then be available in schools away from home. If this is correct, there would then have been a significant decline in the number of suburban students going to a suburban campus without dormitories.

The decline in number of suburban students would probably not have been compensated for by inner-city students if the latter were reluctant to go to a suburban campus because of either the environment or the distance and comparatively poor accessibility by public transportation. The net effect might well have been a sharp drop in enrollment during the 1970s. Something like this may in fact have happened at some of the new suburban campuses built near Chicago or other cities in the late 1960s and early 1970s in anticipation of a permanently high enrollment, which have fallen on difficult times as a result of the decline in enrollment. An inner-city campus would be less susceptible to such difficulty. It would continue to attract students of relatively low-income families, whether these students were of the white ethnic background that the mayor probably expected or of the black and latin background that began to attend college in larger numbers during the late 1960s and the 1970s and found an inner-city campus convenient and attractive.

I would argue, too, that the net social gain from providing higher education for such low-income students is significantly greater than the benefit to be gained from providing an alternative source of higher education for middle-income suburban students. Many students in the former group probably would not have gone to college at all without an inner-city campus; many in the latter group would have gone to some other college if they did not go to the inner-city campus. If this is correct, an inner-city campus would have a better social effect from both its contribution to total income and its contribution to a better distribution of income than would a suburban campus.

In addition to its effects upon the number and character of students, location of the campus in the heart of Chicago may, in my opinion, have contributed to attracting a higher caliber of faculty than would have been the case if the campus has been located in the suburbs. This is contrary to the opinion held by many of the University's representatives at the time when the Miller Meadows and Riverside Golf Club sites were proposed; then it was felt that a suburban site would provide better faculty housing than would an inner-city site and would thus attract a good faculty. However, the nearness of the Chicago Circle Campus to the variety of attractions of the city, cultural and otherwise, and to the intellectual attraction of nearby major universities may have had a positive effect. Those members of the faculty who wish to live in the suburbs and come into the city are easily able to do so at the present location; this might have been more difficult or inconvenient if they both lived and worked in the suburbs under consideration.[1]

I would therefore contend, on the basis of the two arguments above, that the campus is better off in terms of both its quality and attractiveness to potential students as a result of an inner-city rather than a suburban location. At the same time, inner-city graduates probably gain more from their ability and willingness to attend an inner-city campus than would potential graduates of a suburban campus; thus, the net welfare gain to the city and state is larger from an inner-city location than it would have been from a suburban location.

It is believed that Mayor Daley had another intangible gain in mind from placing the campus near the Loop. It is said that he hoped for an extensive interchange between city officials and University faculty, which he felt would contribute significantly to improvement of the city. He had some experience of such interchange with members of

[1]In this statement I may, of course, have generalized to other faculty members my own opinions and feelings. I am informed that this belief runs counter to administrative experience in other urban universities in the country.

the University of Chicago faculty and anticipated the same with the faculty of the University of Illinois. It is difficult to say how much interchange has in fact occurred since 1965, but there probably has not been very much. Associates of the mayor believe it has been less than he had hoped for.

A narrower benefit of an urban campus hoped for by the University would be good relationships with the mayor and the Democratic party organization and support from them in the legislature and other state policy-making agencies. It is difficult to say whether the University has fared better in terms of budget or other issues than would otherwise have been the case without a Chicago campus. However, the mayor's support was important on one major issue: that of separate governance of the Urbana and Chicago campuses considered by a high-level committee of the Illinois Board of Higher Education. Both the administration of the University of Illinois and the Chicago Circle faculty strongly opposed this, as also did Mayor Daley and the City Council. The mayor stated: "There's a movement afoot to relegate the Chicago Circle Campus to a secondary university. We want a full-fledged university." The City Council voted a resolution to protest any change in governance. The issue subsequently died.[2]

These are some of the broader benefits of locating the campus in the inner city. But this location had to be at a specific site, and the choice of Harrison-Halsted had consequences for that neighborhood directly and for the city less directly that must also be considered. In the debate over location of the campus, a major reason offered for placing it in or near the Loop area was that it would serve as an anchor for the Loop, to protect it from deterioration. This was probably the main reason why the mayor strongly preferred the Railway Terminal site just south of the Loop. Although the Harrison-Halsted site did not actually adjoin the Loop as did the Terminal site, its nearness to the Loop was a factor in the final decision to choose that site. The Harrison-Halsted area lay along the western entry to the Loop along the Eisenhower (Congress) Expressway,[3] and location of the Univer-

[2] B. R. Keenan, *Governance of Illinois Higher Education 1945–74*, mutilithed (Urbana: University of Illinois Institute of Government and Public Affairs, 1975), p. 20.

[3] I will be using the present name for both the Eisenhower Expressway (then called Congress) and the Ryan Expressway (then called South).

sity there would help protect that entry from deterioration; further-more, it would provide a southern anchor for the area north of the Eisenhower Expressway to Washington Boulevard and west of the Chicago & North Western and Union stations (an area then and now a skid row) that was planned for future development.

To what extent did location of the campus in the Harrison-Halsted area change that neighborhood and thus contribute to the desired anchoring effect? It is extremely hard to directly measure the anchoring result, since it is not a directly tangible consequence. We will try, however, to use several indirect measures of change in that neighborhood between 1950 and 1970 to get at what might be considered anchoring consequences. It should be clear that we will be comparing the area before and after location of the campus. We will not be making what is the more appropriate, although impossible, comparison: to compare the effects of the University's location in the neighborhood with hypothetical effects of redevelopment plans for the area that had been approved *before* the decision was made to locate the campus there and that were changed by the decision. I do not know what those hypothetical plans would have achieved. I do know that there are sharp differences of opinion on those possible effects, and I will present these later. In summary, there are those who believe the plans would have been successful in developing an area and neighborhood that would have served as a successful example of an integrated residential neighborhood with mixed industrial and commercial uses as well as those who believe the area would have deteriorated badly without the University.

The construction of the University campus did create an island within the city. That island is the area between the Dan Ryan Expressway (or Halsted Street) on the east, Ashland Boulevard and the Medical Center on the west, the Eisenhower Expressway on the north, and Roosevelt Road on the south. Within that area are: (1) the Chicago Circle Campus, about 110 acres built from three urban-renewal projects: Harrison-Halsted, Roosevelt–Blue Island, and half of Congress-Racine; (2) the other half of the Congress-Racine project together with the near West Side conservation project, which had been approved before the University was located in the area;[4] and (3)

---

[4]One of the understandings between city and University when the University accepted the site was that urban renewal would be accelerated in the area between the new campus and the Medical Center.

the Jane Addams Chicago Housing Authority project, which takes up several blocks on the north side of Roosevelt Road and is specifically excluded from the conservation area. Several other high-rise public housing projects exist on the south side of Roosevelt Road, and in the late 1960s the University campus was extended south of Roosevelt Road to include a gym. The area south of Roosevelt Road is not, however, included in my definition of the University island; neither is the Medical Center area west of Ashland. See Map 4 for the area defined.

On the basis of U.S. census data, it is possible to do a comparative static analysis showing this area as it was in three census years: 1950, 1960, and 1970. This area consists of eight census tracts, numbered in 1960: 407, 408, 412 Z, 422, 428, 429, 435, and 436.[5] These tracts extend beyond the campus island to Van Buren Street north of the Eisenhower Expressway. Furthermore, by 1970 almost all of tracts 422 and 436 had been replaced by the University campus. See Map 5 of the tracts.

The population figure for those eight census tracts was 29,105 in 1950. There was a decline in population of about 5,000 from 1950 to 1960, probably as a result of displacements associated with construction of the Eisenhower and Ryan Expressways and the initial clearance of land in the precampus Harrison-Halsted project. But by 1970 there was a far sharper fall to only 10,138. The decline from 1960 to 1970 was due in large part directly to construction of the campus. It has been estimated that more than 8,000 people (in about 1900 families and 650 individual establishments) were displaced by the campus. In addition, another 3,500 were displaced by redevelopment in the near West Side urban-renewal area adjoining the campus. It is probable that another several thousand left either out of fear of future displacement or to accompany family or friends who had been forced out, thus making a total decline in population of about 14,000. In addition to the population loss, the campus displaced approximately

---

[5]While the area is the same, the numbers were somewhat different in 1950 (when tract 421 Z was divided into three tracts, numbered 409, 421, and 430) and in 1970 (when the numbering was 2821–24 and 2831–34). In this study I use the more convenient 1960 numbering from this area for the entire period. Sources for the census data are U.S. Department of Commerce, Bureau of Census: *U.S. Census of Population* (Washington, D.C.: Government Printing Office, 1950): *U.S. Census of Population and Housing* (ibid, 1960 and 1970). All are by census tract.

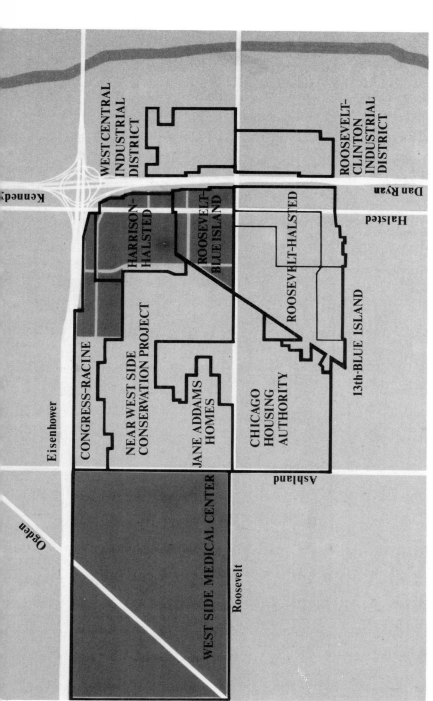

MAP 4 : *University campus site and surrounding neighborhood.*

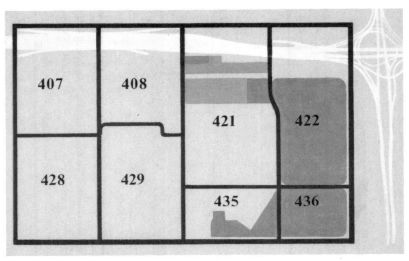

Map 5 : *Census tracts in University campus site and surrounding area.*
Source: *Olcott's Land Values and Zoning* (Chicago: G. C. Olcott & Co., 1961).

630 business units; and another 170 firms were displaced by the West Side urban-renewal program.

The massive exodus of population was accompanied by a significant change in the ethnic character of the population. In 1950, 27,400 whites made up about 95 percent of the 29,000 people living in the eight-tract area; of these approximately one-fourth were foreign-born. Of the foreign-born, over one-half were from Italy, about one-quarter from Mexico, and somewhat less than one-tenth from Greece. The relatively small number of blacks—1,600 or 6 percent of the total population—lived largely in the area along Roosevelt Road, with only a few families in the Jane Addams housing project.

The figures for 1960 are not fully comparable, because the category *foreign-born* was changed to *of foreign stock,* which includes both foreign-born and first-generation (the latter with one foreign-born parent) as distinguished from native. Of the 24,000 remaining in the census area, about 85 percent or 20,500 were white. Of these whites approximately 11,200 were of foreign stock, with 5,100 or 46 percent of these of Italian descent, 4,800 or 43 percent of Mexican origin, and a negligible number of Greek descent. We do not know what percentage of the native stock was of Italian origin in both 1950 and 1960, but it was probably high. The largest percentage increase was in the black population, which more than doubled, rising from 1,600 in 1950 to 3,500 in 1960, an increase that amounted to 15 percent of the smaller total. The main reason for this rise was an increase in black occupancy of the Jane Addams housing project (which forms the largest part of tract 429). Whereas blacks occupied 58 housing units in that tract in 1950, they occupied 720 units—well over half the total units—in that tract in 1960. Blacks also occupied about 250 housing units in the two census tracts adjoining 429.

In 1970 the population was far smaller. The greatest decline was concentrated in the white population, although all groups had declined. Of the 10,000 still living in the area, only about 6,800 were white; of these over half were of foreign stock, and of the foreign stock 1,800 or 48 percent were of Italian origin, and 1,300 or 34 percent were of Mexican origin. Approximately 3,500 persons of Mexican origin and 3,300 of Italian origin had been displaced. But, if it is assumed that a significant proportion of the native-born whites were of Italian origin—since Italians had been in the area for many

generations, whereas Mexicans had been there for one or two generations at most—the population of Italian origin would still remain as
half, if not more, of the total white population, whereas the Mexican
proportion would have declined to about 15–20 percent. The smallest
decline was in the black population, which fell from about 3,500 in
1960 to 2,900, so that in 1970 the black population had reached about
29 percent of the total.

What was very significant, however, was the change in location of
the blacks in the area. Previously they had occupied a small but
significant number of housing units outside tract 429, which contains
the Jane Addams housing project; but now they were almost entirely
concentrated in that one tract. Conversely, the number of housing
units occupied by whites in that tract had fallen sharply. By 1970 the
project had not only become almost entirely black, a process which
continued until full black occupancy was reached during the 1970s,
but the blacks in the entire area were now contained in that project and
tract. (Blacks were and are a large part of the population in the public
housing projects south of Roosevelt Road, and both blacks and latins
are a large part of the population in the Pilsen area also to the south.)
Many people in the area consider the concentration of blacks in the
Addams project a result of either a deliberate or misguided Chicago
Housing Authority policy. As the income of white residents in the
Addams project rose above the public-housing maximum, the law
was interpreted in such a fashion that those whites were forced out
and replaced by low-income blacks, with no effort made to achieve a
racial balance within the project.

With the decline in population and the demolition of structures that
accompanied construction of the campus and the conservation plan,
the housing stock also fell sharply. In 1950 there were about 7,300
units, in 1960 approximately 6,850, and in 1970 only 3,400. During
the 1930s the Jane Addams housing project was almost the only
housing built, and during the 1940s there had been no housing
construction. Of those units for which data were available in 1950,
over 80 percent were built before 1919; and of the reporting units, 14
percent had no running water or were dilapidated and another 13
percent had no private bath. Fourteen percent were owner-occupied,
84 percent were renter-occupied, and 2 percent were vacant.

The 1960 census found that 98 percent of the homes were built before 1939, that there was almost no construction during the 1950s, and that the proportions by types of occupancy were about the same as in 1950. While the quality measures were not comparable, it is significant that the census found 70 percent of the housing units in sound condition and classified only 30 percent as deteriorating or dilapidated. Interestingly, those census tracts with above-average proportions of deteriorating and dilapidated housing were the tract containing the Harrison-Halsted project, which had been recognized when the area had been designated a Land Clearance Commission project in 1956; the tract adjoining it, which subsequently became the Roosevelt–Blue Island project; and some parts of the tracts that became the Congress-Racine project (but other tracts included in the latter project area were rated high in terms of quality). The quality of housing found by the census examiners seems to have been somewhat higher than that subsequently found by the city when it determined the areas were "slum and blighted areas" suitable for demolition.

By 1970, after the campus had been built and the conservation program was underway, a sharp fall in the stock of old housing is indicated. The stock of pre-1930 housing fell from about 6,000 units in 1960 to 2,600 units in 1970 (about equal to the total decline in housing stock). Although construction figures for the 1970 census seem to have been determined on a different basis from those of earlier census years, since they show greater construction in the decades of the 1940s and 1950s than are shown in the 1950 and 1960 censuses, the figures in all cases are small. It is significant, however, that more than 160 housing units were built in the decade of the 1960s, a higher figure than was shown in the previous two decades by any census. It is also a sign of the concentration of blacks in the Jane Addams units that occurred in the decade of the 1960s that the proportion of black renters to the smaller total number of renters in the area rose substantially from 1960 to 1970, and the number of black owner-occupied houses, while small in both 1960 and 1970, fell very sharply in that same decade.

In addition to the fall in population and housing stock, there was, as might be expected, a sharp decline in number of workers residing in the area. The resident civilian labor force fell from more than 11,000 workers in 1950 to 8,500 in 1960 and 3,900 in 1970. The great fall occurred in the number of private wage and salary workers, with a smaller decrease in the number of self-employed; government workers increased somewhat. This change in character of employment was in part a consequence of the departure of many previous residents and the rezoning of the neighborhood so that industrial plants and trucking firms were eliminated south of the Eisenhower Expressway. In addition, some of the old residents found jobs at the new campus, and the new residents who moved in worked at the new campus, the Medical Center, in government offices in the Loop, or in other nearby areas. This change in employment in the area from 1960 to 1970 is brought out clearly in Table 1.

The different structure of occupations was associated with a significant upward movement in the average income of family and unrelated individuals living in this area. In 1950 the median income of this group of residents was in the $2,000 to $2,999 income class; in 1960 it was in the $4,000 to $4,999 income class; and by 1970, in the six noncampus tracts, it was in the $7,000 to $7,999 income class. If census tract 429, in which the Jane Addams housing project is located, is excluded, the apparent increase is even greater. In 1950,

TABLE 1 : *Employment in the Area, 1960 and 1970**

INDUSTRY CLASS	1960	%	1970	%
Construction	310	4.0	110	3.0
Manufacturing	2769	35.4	1096	29.5
Transportation	616	7.9	168	4.5
Communications, utilities, and sanitation	161	2.1	124	3.3
Wholesale trade	240	3.1	105	2.8
Retail trade	1067	13.6	429	11.6
Health services	218	2.8	337	9.1
Educational services	169	2.2	248	6.7
Other services	587	7.5	840	22.6
Other industry (including *not reported*)	1687	21.6	256	6.9
Total	7824	100.0	3713	100.0

*In 1960, included those over 14 years of age; in 1970, those over 16 years.
Source: U.S., Department of Commerce, Bureau of the Census, *U.S. Census of Population and Housing* (Washington, D.C.: Government Printing Office, 1960 and 1970).

when the Addams project was largely occupied by whites, the median income in that tract was about equal to that in the seven other tracts. In 1960, when over 50 percent of the population in that tract was black, the median income in that tract was about 50 percent of that in the other tracts; in 1970, when that tract was almost entirely populated by blacks, the median income there was less than 50 percent of that in the other tracts. In census tracts 407 and 408, bounded by Racine, Polk, Ashland, and Van Buren (which, of course, excludes the Addams project), and in tract 421 Z, bounded by Morgan, Van Buren, Racine, and Taylor streets—i.e., those three tracts in which the population is white and largely of Italian origin—the median income of families and unrelated individuals rose by about 50 to 60 percent from 1950 to 1960 and then by another 100 percent from 1960 to 1970, so that over those twenty years the average income level more than tripled. Not surprisingly, accompanying that shift in occupations and the rise in average income, the median number of school years completed by an individual rose from about 8 to 10 years, with a somewhat greater length of schooling in the Italian tracts. (A change in age of employment would also have contributed to this last phenomenon.)

One of the most significant measures of improvement in an area is the change in land values over a period of time. Olcott's *Land Values and Zoning* provides data over that period with respect to changes in land values of representative plots of land in the eight census tracts and an adjoining area. The data are given in Table 2.

Prior to the offer of the Harrison-Halsted area to the University in late 1960 and the University's acceptance in Febraury 1961, the only tract in the area to show a significant increase in land values from 1950 to 1961 was tract 422, where the Harrison-Halsted project was underway. The rise in values there may have reflected expectations from the redevelopment begun in that area, the improvements taking place, and the efforts of the Near West Side Planning Board to find a developer. Other than in that one tract, changes in land values were slight. However, from 1961 to 1965 land values approximately doubled and then doubled again from 1965 to 1971 in those tracts not occupied by the new campus or the Campus Green development. Since then values seem to have 'remained constant. I am told by knowledgeable persons that there was little if any market for land in the area before 1961.

TABLE 2 : *Changing Land Values of Selected Plots of Land**
in the Eight Census Tracts and an Adjoining Area from 1950 to 1977
(in dollars per front foot, 125 feet in depth)

	407	408	421	422	428	429	435	436	JACKSON–ASHLAND AREA
1950	$ 40	$ 35	$ 45	$ 45	$ 35	$ 35	$ 35	$ 40	$110
1955	40	35	55	65	35	35	40	50	150
1960	45	40	55	65	45	40	40	50	150
1961	55	50	65	75	55	50	50	70	175
1963	65	60	65	75	65	60	60	70	175
1965	110	110	110	Univ.	90	90	100	Univ.	200
				Campus				Campus	
1967	125	125	125		100	100	100		200
1969	Campus Green	150	150		150	150	150		200
1971		200	200		200	200	200		200
1977		200	200		200	200	200		200

*In developing the data used in this table the land value for a representative plot of land in a tract was selected. Corner plots of land are more expensive; an interior plot in a tract was selected for this table, since such a plot is closer to the average, and would sell at an average price.

Source: *Olcott's Land Values Blue Book* (Chicago: G. C. Olcott & Co., for each year).

After 1963, once the legal suits against construction of the campus had been decided so that the University construction could proceed and the city went ahead with its spending in the near West Side conservancy area, there was a change in expectations about this area among developers and individuals; it became a good area in which to buy land. It was believed that land values had bottomed out and would rise in the future. Developers such as Talman Savings and Loan and Baird and Warner, which helped finance Westgate Terrace and Campus Green respectively, were among the first. In addition, some individuals began to buy homes, either as a long-term investment or for speculative resale, from people who wanted to sell out of fear when the University came into the area.

The open market has been largely dominated by larger sales of land on the part of the Department of Urban Renewal at prices above a minimum, and it is those minimum prices that Olcott's probably shows after 1971.[6] (The constancy of land prices since 1971 is somewhat surprising, because prices of homes have risen significantly over the same period.) There has apparently been little in the way of private sales of land on the open market in the area since 1970. Few plots of land come onto the open market, and it is said that most sales and purchases are held within the Italian community without public announcement. Table 2 also shows that land values in the campus area rose far more rapidly than did those in the nearby Jackson-Ashland district, where they started at a much higher figure but leveled off at $200.

Another comparison is made of changes in land values within the campus area with land values in three other parts of the city with populations somewhat comparable to that in the campus district. The land values in the three areas are shown in Table 3. These districts are also inhabited by a largely white population, many of foreign origin, with a high percentage employed in blue-collar occupations at

---

[6]Some data are available for sale prices of Department of Urban Renewal land plots over time. In 1965 the site for Westgate sold for $0.88 per square foot (although one bid was as high as $1.31). In 1968 the three sites for Campus Green sold for $1.20, $1.80, and $1.85 per square foot. In 1970 the site for Circle Court Shopping Center sold for $2.08 per square foot (although one bid was as high as $2.80). In 1977 a plot at Vernon Park and Carpenter streets for single family housing sold for $2.00 per square foot. Department of Urban Renewal, *Near West Side News*, vol. 3 (December 1965), p. 2; vol. 6 (January 1968), p. 3; vol. 8 (June 1970), p. 3; and *Urban Renewal Notice*, vol. 16 (December 1977), p. 4.

TABLE 3 : *Changing Land Values in Four Other Census Tracts in Chicago, 1950 to 1970*
(in dollars per front foot, 125 feet in depth)

| YEAR | CENSUS TRACT NUMBERS | | | |
	186 IRVING PARK	765 BRIDGEPORT	264 LOGAN SQUARE	383 VAN BUREN AND WESTERN
1950	$ 35	$ 15	$ 50	$ 35
1955	42	27	60	35
1960	100	50	85	40
1961	100	65	85	40
1963	125	85	110	60
1965	150	115	135	100
1967	200	125	150	115
1969	200	125	150	115
1971	250	125	125	115
1977	250	125	100	75

Irving Park in 1960 had a population that was 55% of foreign stock, with Germany, Poland, and Italy the main countries of origin.

Bridgeport in 1960 had a population that was 41% of foreign stock, with Poland, Mexico, Italy, and Lithuania the main countries of origin.

Logan Square in 1960 had a population that was 49% of foreign stock, with Poland by far the main country of origin and Germany second.

Van Buren and Western in 1960 had a population that was over 75% black.

Source: Bureau of the Census, *U.S. Census of Population and Housing* (1960); and *Olcott's Land Values Blue Book*.

income levels somewhat higher than but comparable to those of the Italian population in the Circle Campus area. Data for a fourth district in a nearby census tract that had become largely black by 1960 are also presented in that table.

In the largely black-populated tract west of the campus, land values peaked in 1967 to a figure comparable to that in the campus district, but thereafter declined sharply. In the Bridgeport and Logan Square tracts, land values rose in a fashion similar to that in the campus area until 1967; then in Bridgeport they remained stable at a lower figure than they reached in the campus area, whereas in Logan Square they declined after 1969. The Irving Park tract shows an overall greater rise than the campus district since 1950, but between 1960 and 1977 the increase in the campus area was about 300 percent and in Irving Park only 150 percent. This comparison supports the conclusion that land values in the campus area west of the Circle Campus rose both more rapidly and to a higher level than they would have without the campus, without considering as an alternative the hypothetical effects of the neighborhood's own unfulfilled development plans.

In summary, this comparative static analysis indicates that the construction of the campus and the carrying out of the near West Side urban-renewal plan did have a major result that the city desired: it created an island of higher incomes and land values along one of the major entrances to the Loop, along the Eisenhower Expressway. The area of the island situated between two major campuses of the University of Illinois—the Chicago Circle Campus and the Medical Center Campus—had experienced a major reduction in population, a major shift in economic character away from industry, a significant increase in family income, and a significant increase in land values.

The term *deterioration* as applied to an area is often a polite cover for the massive entry of black and latin populations into an area; and one rationale for the proposed construction of the campus in both the South Loop and Garfield Park areas was that it would slow down such deterioration. If this was also an unstated aim for location of the campus at the Harrison-Halsted site, it had that result. As Map 6 shows, the further movement of blacks into the area from Roosevelt Road to the Eisenhower Expressway between Ashland and Halsted was stopped and contained. It was stopped in the sense that no additional blacks entered the area, and it was contained in the sense that all blacks living in the area were confined to the Jane Addams project.[7] With respect to the latin population, there was a sharp decline in the number of residents of Mexican or Puerto Rican origin in the area. The net consequence was to strengthen the relative position of the population of Italian origin that had remained in the area, even though the number of persons of Italian origin had declined sharply. While many new residents of all types moved into new developments in the area, the political dominance of the Italian

[7] A recent map of areas of black residence in Chicago in 1977 (see Map 6) shows this clearly. In this map, except for the University island, both sides of the western corridor into the Loop along the Eisenhower Expressway were 75 percent or more black in 1977 and had reached that proportion in 1970. (That includes the West Garfield Park area.)

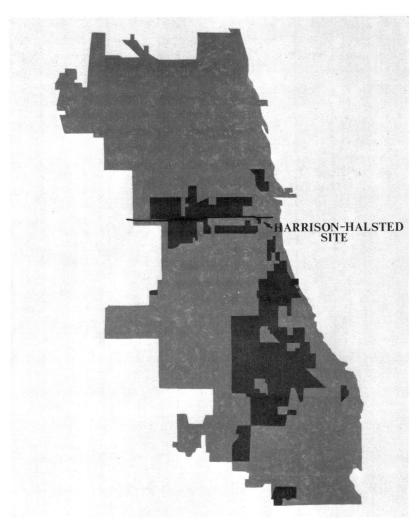

MAP 6 : *Areas of black residence in Chicago, 1977.*
Source: *Chicago Tribune,* May 26, 1978, sec. 1, p. 3.

group, which had controlled the 1st Ward for many years, may have been strengthened by the changes that occurred since 1960.

Up to this point we have looked at this change as a series of snapshots taken in particular years. Can we say anything of the dynamic factors that led to those results? It is possible, based upon city files on the three projects that made up the campus site, to make an estimate of the number of families and businesses displaced by the campus. (These figures often vary slightly from one file to another, but these slight variations do not change the total picture significantly.) About 1,900 families, averaging 4 persons per family, and over 650 single individuals were displaced. Approximately 630 businesses were forced out: 200 from the Harrison-Halsted project area, 270 from Roosevelt–Blue Island, and 160 from Congress-Racine. Many were small neighborhood establishments rooted in the area, so that of the 630 displaced about 200 preferred to close down rather than move. In addition, another 848 families and 273 single residents, as well as 174 business firms, were displaced by the Near West Side Urban Renewal project. Of the latter businesses, 57 discontinued operation rather than move. (Approximately 45 percent of the displaced families and 33 percent of the single residents in the Congress-Racine project area and the Near West Side Urban Renewal project area were Spanish speaking.) Of the business firms that continued operation but in another location, well over 90 percent remained within Chicago. The largest firms to move from the area were John M. Smyth Furniture, Paris Garter, and Flex-Rite; but many smaller industrial firms, producing a wide variety of products such as luggage, biscuits, bags, textiles, lamps, and religious articles, and trading firms selling an even greater variety of products or services at both wholesale and retail were also displaced. In addition to the businesses, several institutions closed or moved. The most famous of these was Hull-House, the future of which stirred a national reaction; others, the closing of which sparked neighborhood reaction, included the Holy Guardian Angel Church and its school, the Catholic Youth Organization, and several schools. It was estimated in testimony before the City Council Committee on Housing and Planning that the tax loss in this area, based on existing use only, as a result of the demolition of property to construct the campus was approximately

$1.0 million per year in real estate taxes; but the method of making that estimate was not described.[8]

Substantial amounts were invested in the area. The University, the city, and the federal government combined to spend $27 million to purchase the campus land. In addition, the University constructed the campus buildings for an additional investment of $150–$200 million.[9]

This University-associated investment by federal, state, and local governments created the Circle Campus and thereby the island for redevelopment between the Circle Campus and the Medical Center. Within this island the city and the federal government combined to spend about $15 million for redevelopment for residential and limited commercial use.[10] This latter investment permitted widening and resurfacing of many of the area's major streets, widespread planting of trees, beautification of smaller streets, creation of additional park and play space, and expansion of institutional facilities. The federal portion of $10 million was used to buy up dilapidated and nonconforming structures for demolition, and land thus acquired was resold to developers by the Department of Urban Renewal.

Private developers have come into the area.[11] They have invested about $23 million. Five residential projects have been or are now being built, with 560 new and currently occupied housing units and another 300 units now under construction or committed. It is expected that two of these five projects will expand by later stages, with a further investment estimated at more than $30 million, to build another 300 housing units. Much of this investment has been financed by Federal Housing Authority loans made available to developers at very favorable terms. In addition to residential development, approx-

---

[8]T. J. Haring, planning consultant to the Harrison-Halsted Community Group, statement made before the City Council Committee on Housing and Planning, April 13, 1961, mimeographed, p. 4. Scala Papers.

[9]See infra, ch. 8, p. 162, for a breakdown of land purchase cost; see also Board of Trustees, *Minutes* (Trustees' Papers): July 26, 1960, pp. 73–83; July 27, 1966, pp. 23–26.

[10]See Department of Urban Renewal, *Near West Side Urban Renewal Plan* (Chicago: City of Chicago, 1969), p. 7. (This excludes Medical Center Commission expenditures and proceeds from land sales.)

[11]Data in this and the next six paragraphs are based on interviews in the neighborhood.

imately $5–$8 million was invested for the Circle Court Shopping
Center by the Republic National Bank and various buyers of space in
that center, the most important of which are the bank itself and a
Jewel grocery store. That Jewel store is considered to be one of the
most successful inner-city supermarkets in Chicago, and its success
has encouraged Jewel to invest in other inner-city stores. Some stores
among the first group to occupy the center were not successful and
have been replaced by offices and other stores.

Perhaps of equal significance, in that it shows the attitude of area
homeowners, is the large investment by area residents in their own
homes and businesses. The Department of Urban Renewal estimates
on a conservative basis that homeowners have invested $5 million of
their own funds in the improvement of their homes and have bor-
rowed another $1.5 million for home rehabilitation on very favorable
terms under Section 312 of the Housing Act. Local businessmen have
also invested an estimated $.5 million to improve their business
facilities. The new residential developments are all fully occupied;
and, as far as I can gather, few properties in the area are for sale, and
few housing units are vacant. The Department of Urban Renewal still
has one large vacant site—a plot on the northeast corner of Roosevelt
and Ashland—for which it is seeking a developer, and it is hoped that
one will soon be found. (See Map 7 for outline of the Near West Side
Conservation Project.)

Housing prices and rentals in the area have apparently gone up,
judging by illustrative figures of purchase prices and rentals in the
new private developments. In Westgate Terrace a 3–4 bedroom
townhouse sold for $23,500 to $27,000 in 1965; the price of similar
housing in 1977 ranged from $60,000 to $70,000 for the most recent
sales. That project has shown the highest price rise. In the Circle
Square project the price of 3–4 bedroom townhouses was set at about
$28,000 to $29,000 on construction in 1967; the current price is
estimated at about $50,000. Campus Green townhouses were built in
1967 to sell at about $28,000 to $31,000; by the time Baird and
Warner had sold the last one some years back, the prices were close to
$55,000. The first twenty Garden Court townhouses built by Joseph
Cacciatore and Company sold in a range of $50,000 to $61,000 in
1975 when the first phase of the development was completed, but the
second twenty now under construction are expected to sell for at least

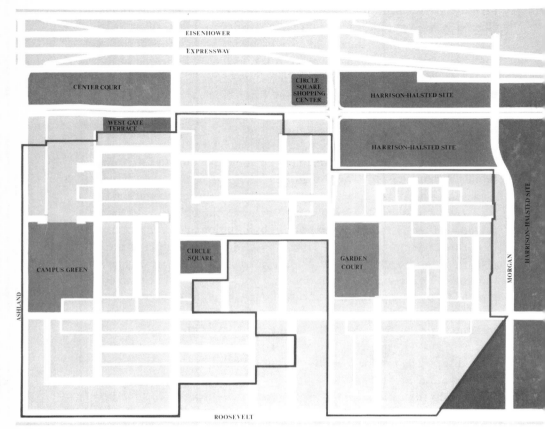

MAP 7 : *Near West Side Conservation Project, 1967.*

10 percent more. C. H. Shaw Company plans to build townhouses in the later stage of its construction program and anticipates that, when these are offered for sale some years in the future, prices will exceed $75,000. (In this paragraph *current* and *most recent* mean *as of 1978.*)

Rents have risen even more. In the Campus Green project, studio to two-bedroom apartments rented within a range of $95 to $270 per month when that project was opened in 1968; by 1978 the monthly rents for an average studio or one-bedroom on a middle-level floor were in the $275 to $320 range. C. H. Shaw expects to rent its studio and one-bedroom apartments within a range of $225 to $325, with two-bedrooms going for $400; and in Westgate the apartment rentals in duplexes range from $350 to $450 per month. While such figures are only illustrative, they do show that the price of housing over the past ten years has increased by about 75–150 percent in the new developments in the area, although there are variations depending on the specific location and type of housing.

The people who have occupied these new developments are only in part from the University. It is my impression that from within the University the Medical Center faculty, staff, and students have provided a greater number of buyers and tenants for the new developments than have the same groups from the Chicago Circle Campus. This is especially true of the Campus Green apartments, which were designed with the students, younger staff, and faculty of the Medical Center and nearby hospitals in mind; it will probably be true also for the new Center Court development of C. H. Shaw, which, in its first phase, is directed toward a similar group of tenants. Other developments have attracted some people employed by the University, but they have also attracted families and individuals from other parts of the city, who for one reason or another prefer the near West Side. It may be for convenience to work in the Loop or for other advantages of a near-Loop location; it may be that other sections of the city, such as the near North Side, with comparable living space have simply become too expensive or have gone into condominiums, so that the near West Side is now considered a good value; and, finally, it may be that this area still has a quality of neighborhood that the new residents enjoy.

Only a few of the new owners or tenants seem to have come from the suburbs; many are described as college-trained professionals; and frequently both the husband and wife are working. After the city introduced the requirement that city employees must live in the city, the developments attracted some of these. In one of the developments it was estimated that the average family income is in the $20,000 to $25,000 range; but while this was more an educated guess than a factual statistic, it seems reasonable enough to be projected beyond that one development. All of the developments are described as having an international flavor, which generally means they have a significant number of Asian residents, who tend to be associated with the Medical Center. They also have, or try to attract, black and latin residents; but in this they have not been very successful. The most serious difficulty in attracting more of these is the high cost of space in the new developments in relation to family incomes within those groups.

In discussing the area's development, mention should also be made of the low-income project which still exists in the area and of one other similar attempted project. The Jane Addams project remains a Chicago Housing Authority public housing project and is fully occupied by blacks paying heavily subsidized rents. The leaders of the residents in that project are fearful that the land and housing have become so valuable that efforts will be made to force the present occupants out of the project, and to replace them with higher-income residents paying market rents for the area. The housing in this project is attractive, being low-rise and well-constructed; it is far better designed than are the later high-rise public-housing projects. Some of the leaders of the area's white community consider Addams project a disadvantage to the neighborhood; the leaders of the black community realize that low-income housing may not be compatible with high-value land. But all are aware that it would not be easy to find any housing, public or private, for the present low-income residents of the Addams project should they be forced out and that whatever alternative housing was found would almost certainly not be as good. Thus, while there is loose talk of changing the status of this public-housing project, it is almost certain that to do so would cause serious difficulties, which would require a political decision at the highest level of city administration. For the near future at least, the political costs of such a move appear to be so high that any change is unlikely.

Some years ago a latin group attempted to bid for cleared land to construct low-income housing for latin residents in the area. However, at the last minute, before this group could bid, the main financial backer for the proposed project withdrew its support, and the group no longer had the capacity to bid for the land. There were charges that the proposed backer was pressured into withdrawing the promised support, and the latin group sued claiming discrimination. After three years of court battle, the suit was dismissed. There was then and is still a serious doubt whether construction of low-income housing would be economically feasible in this area without heavy subsidization, quite apart from the difficulties of financing and other problems the latin group faced. The land in question was sold to another developer with plans for higher-income housing that was more compatible with other developments in the area. Clearly, however, this result supported the higher-income use of the land and the maintenance of the area as a higher-income island.[12]

While on the surface the campus itself does not appear to have much direct economic impact on the neighborhood other than bounding the area,[13] a closer look indicates this is somewhat deceptive. During the fall quarters of the three most recent academic years, approximately 275–300 students lived in the neighborhood. One of the neighborhood leaders guesses that roughly about 50 students from homes in the neighborhood have been going to college each year at Circle Campus (many of whom might not have gone without the campus). If that is so, approximately 200–250 students come to live there from outside the area while they are going to the University. While living in the neighborhood, the expenditures of these students for housing, food, and other necessities represent a net contribution to the area's income. If the spending per student is crudely estimated

[12]"Urban Renewal Poses Some Hard Choices," *New York Times,* April 21, 1978, p. D-15, states that a shift of inner-city land from lower-income to higher-income housing uses is occuring in many cities in the country. Washington, D.C., San Francisco, Philadelphia, Baltimore, and Houston are mentioned as cities where this has occurred already or where it may occur in the near future.

[13]Defined for the following two paragraphs as the region covered by postal zip code 60607 in the University records of home addresses. The material on residency was supplied by the office of administrative and information services at Circle Campus. This discussion excludes the impact of the campus construction during the period 1963–70.

at $2,000 per year, the total amount of additional expenditures in the area is about $500,000, of which somewhat less would be an addition to income. (This is a net addition to the area's income but not to the city's if these students would have spent those funds in other parts of the city from which they may have come.)

During the same period, an average of 65 Chicago Circle staff members—academic and nonacademic—lived in the area. Of these about 35 were nonacademic. If it is assumed that about 20 of these nonacademic employees lived in the area permanently and would have worked elsewhere if not at Chicago Circle, then the other 45 are people who moved into the area because they worked at the University (and would have lived elsewhere had they worked elsewhere). The income of these 45 employees and their families is a net addition to the area's income that would not have arisen except for the campus; in turn those 45, by their spending in the area, raise the income of the local merchants, homeowners, and others. If it is conservatively assumed that the average family income of each of these campus employees is about $20,000, then their total contribution to the area's income from their employment is $900,000. In addition, I will assume that each of these families spends 20 percent of its income in the area for rent and purchases from local businessmen and that of these expenditures half remains as income for neighborhood residents and businesses. This would add another $90,000 of income to area residents, resulting in a total contribution of about $1 million to the area's income by this group. (Again, this is not an increase in city income if these residents would have lived in the city anyway had the campus been located elsewhere.)

A final source of income generated by the campus arises from the 20,000 transients students, faculty, and staff who spend from 4–8 hours per weekday in the area. If it is conservatively estimated that each of these spends $1 per week in an area business, their total expenditures during a year would be about $1 million, although their contribution to the area's income would be lower, say by half, since some of the money spent in the area would leak out. Thus, the value of the additional income to the area directly and indirectly created by students, faculty, and staff in the above three groups totals approximately $2 million. This is apart from any addition to income created

Campus construction 1963–64. UICC ARCHIVES.

The area west of Circle Campus facing the Medical Center complex, looking from University Hall (1976). ASHISH K. SEN PHOTOGRAPH.

An example of the University architecture, the Behavioral Sciences Building, with one of the University's several parking lots to the west.
ASHISH K. SEN PHOTOGRAPH.

Garden Court townhouses (1980). FRANK O. WILLIAMS PHOTOGRAPH.

by the University's own spending in the area for supplies and services or from the spending of non-University people who may be visiting the area because the campus is there.

The 1970 census figures given earlier show a significant rise in average per-family incomes in the area from 1960 to 1970. This rise was much greater for the white population than for the black. The previous discussion makes it possible to identify two of the reasons for the rise: one is the movement into the area of many comparatively higher-income residents and the consequent movement out of lower-income residents whose homes were cleared. (Most of the housing units in the new developments were opened after the 1970 census was taken, so the 1980 census should show an even greater increase.) The other reason is the direct income generated by the Circle Campus, quite apart from that arising from the Medical Center, the income-generating effects of which are probably even greater for the area.

But the censuses show that these effects are largely confined to the area's white population. Few, if any, businesses in the area are black-owned. Almost all the 1,000 black families estimated to be living in the area as of 1978 live in the Jane Addams houses. The main breadwinner in about 70 percent of those families is unemployed, and an even larger percentage of those families is on welfare. Many of these families have been in the project for some time, and the fact that they remain there indicates that their incomes have not risen above the maximum figure permitted for residents of such projects and that their gains from the campus are minimal.[14]

Apart from the direct employment and income-generating effects of the campus, its location has probably had another beneficial effect on the area. As mentioned earlier, on the basis of a very rough guess, as many as 50 young people from the area may be attending college at Chicago Circle at any one time. While some of these would have gone to college anyway, regardless of the location of Circle Campus, others have gone because the campus is where it is. This tendency seems to be strongest among potential students of Italian origin, but it also seems to be true in the past few years of potential Spanish-

---

[14]It may be true that black residents of the Jane Addams project would be unable to work for the University at its pay scale and retain their homes, since they might then rise above the maximum allowable income limits. If this is so, it would appear to be a *Catch-22* situation that insures against residents of the project gaining from the campus by university employment.

speaking students. I gather this may be less true of potential black students in the area: very good black students can go to college anywhere in the country, whereas those who have less choice or wish to stay in Chicago prefer to attend Malcolm X.

I have, up to now, given some indication of various positive results that arose from the location of the campus in the city. Many of these are intangible and few are measurable or additive. But the campus's location also had negative consequences, not so much for the University as for the neighborhood and, perhaps indirectly, for the city. These consequences are even less tangible than are the benefits that may have arisen from the location. I have already mentioned one of these: the one-sided overriding of almost fifteen years of planning and work by the neighborhood groups that were seeking to redevelop their neighborhood along lines they felt desirable and appropriate. Many of those who were themselves involved in the planning obviously felt betrayed or dismayed, but others who were not actively involved in the planning had similar feelings. They may have contributed to the new Holy Guardian Angel Church, improved their homes or beautified their street or alley with the city's encouragement, been planning to buy a home in the Harrison-Halsted residential redevelopment, or have had a small business. Then they were forced out, some receiving adequate financial compensation but many not, especially if a local business had been condemned. It was the women of this latter group who brought Florence Scala into the fight and who actively supported the struggle against the campus.

Many residents of the area before 1961, whom I interviewed, described the neighborhood as it was then as a "good one." The people knew each other and watched out for each other; crime was described as slight, since they recognized strangers. It was possible to bring up children well according to community standards. There seemed to be in general at least tolerable, and in individual cases friendly, relations among different ethnic groups. Older residents had families and friends nearby and appreciated the stability.

This older quality of the neighborhood was largely changed by the campus and related developments. Those people who moved away still remember the area fondly, and there are even reunions among people of the same ethnic groups. They consider the end of the neighborhood a major loss. Several of those who moved used almost the same words to say that if the city were to attempt something similar where they now live they would lead the fight against it. In at least one case a person who said this did lead such a fight successfully in another neighborhood.

The people who remember this take the position that the neighborhood would have redeveloped successfully without the campus on the basis of the Planning Board's plans. It would have been an example of an integrated neighborhood, with residents of Italian, Mexican, Puerto Rican, and Greek origin living together successfully with the blacks. They argue that the unity displayed by these same people in the fight against the University supports this possibility. The development of an area that was residential but also included other uses, such as clean industries and businesses, would have combined jobs and good housing near each other and would have yielded to the city revenues that would have supported the amenities of the neighborhood. The closeness of the area to the Loop by CTA and the expressways would have made it attractive for both homebuyers and businesses.

Placing the University there removed from revenue-yielding uses some of the most potentially valuable land in the city. It was estimated that, as a result of the campus's placement, the total loss in real estate taxes is about $2 million annually in comparison with revenues that would have been derived from the uses originally planned. At the same time, approximately 5,000 potential inner-city dwelling units that would have been built had the original plans come to fruition were eliminated.[15] The loss of revenue-yielding land would contribute to, rather than solve, the financial problems of the inner city.

Those city officials, outsiders such as news reporters, and even a few area people who favored the University's location at Harrison-Halsted spoke in almost diametrically opposite terms. They considered the district a poor one with further decline threatened. The quality of much of the housing was low, the zoning mix was undesirable, the streets were dangerous with filfth underfoot, petty crime was serious, and the area had more of the characteristics of a gangs-

[15]See Haring, statement before City Council Committee on Housing and Planning, p. 4. This is different from the $1 million figure cited earlier, which is based on loss of revenue from *existing* rather than *potential* land use. The basis of these figures is not given.

ter-dominated slum than a well-functioning, integrated neighborhood. Perhaps more than that, they were skeptical about the success
of the redevelopment plans. They saw the area deteriorating further
and becoming more and more like the crumbling districts south of
Roosevelt Road. Many of these also felt, and at times argued, that
residents of a neighborhood always oppose redevelopment, and decision-makers must consider the larger issue of what is good for the
whole community rather than the small neighborhood.[16] They also
argued that many people who were forced out would have been
forced out later anyway as the area deteriorated further; and they
claimed that many of the younger residents welcomed the money they
got from the condemnation of their homes or businesses, because this
enabled them to move elsewhere.

In my interviews, those who presented the optimistic scenario
described above were often criticized as being nostalgic, while those
who presented the pessimistic result were criticized for rationalizing
the decision. I am neither interested in deciding which view is correct
nor able to do so without much greater knowledge of the neighborhood as it was before 1961 than I now have or can get. But, clearly, if
the first group is correct, the intangible costs derived from location of
the University there are very high; if the second group is correct, the
intangible costs are low.[17] In the latter case, the costs arise in part
from the displacement of people, especially the elderly, and from the
displacement and closing of businesses.

Under any circumstances the methods adopted by the mayor
alerted other neighborhoods to the possibility or threat of urban
renewal over the objections of people living there. It is claimed that
Florence Scala and her group established a model of protest and
sit-ins that would be used subsequently in other areas. Again, for

[16]See, for example, Hull-House Board of Trustees, *Minutes,* February 23, 1961 (Scala
Papers), remarks made by Anthony Downs during debate on the location issue.

[17]For a comparison of similarly varying perceptions that accompanied redevelopment of an
Italian neighborhood in the West End of Boston that seems to bear a marked resemblance to the
Harrison-Halsted neighborhood, see Herbert J. Gans, *Urban Villagers* (New York: Free Press,
1962). Gans discusses redevelopment of the area in ch. 13 especially; for different perceptions
of the area—whether it was a slum or low-rent district—by outsiders and insiders, see pp.
308–17. Similarly, Theordore J. Lowi and Benjamin Ginsberg, *Poliscide,* ch. 9, point out
different perceptions of an area in Weston, Illinois, held by inhabitants of the area and by county
and state officials engaged in its clearance and redevelopment.

those protesting, the model may be an effective one, although outsiders may feel it is unseemly and undemocratic. If, however, there is no other way to prevent a unilateral action by the city, little other choice of means to resist may be available. The mayor's success in the Harrison-Halsted area may have subsequently made it more difficult for the city to carry out other "desirable" urban renewal programs by making the residents more alert to such a threat and thus bringing about more neighborhood participation before a redevelopment plan.

This, however, I do not consider a cost; it may in fact be a benefit. As pointed out, an immediate consequence claimed by opponents of the campus was the defeat in 1962 of a local bond issue, strongly supported by the mayor, for funds for redevelopment.[18] How costly this would be would depend on whether other funds became available or if the desired funds were voted later. If either or both had happened, the economic cost would have been low, although the mayor's prestige may have been reduced temporarily. For his part, the mayor regarded the campus as a positive factor in his tough but successful campaign for re-election in 1963, and he urged that construction be sped up so that he could show visible evidence of progress.

Another frequently mentioned cost is the closing of Hull-House in the neighborhood and demolition of most of its buildings. It is at least questionable whether Hull-House could or should have remained in the area. The buildings were old and most of them required major repairs. In addition, as incomes in the area rose and the first generation population fell in numbers, Hull-House was increasingly uncertain of its proper work in the neighborhood. The money received by Hull-House for the buildings permitted a move elsewhere and a greater decentralization of effort than had existed before. It also saved the cost of the major fund-raising effort that would have been required if it had remained where it was. Finally, the University memorialized Hull-House by rebuilding two of its old buildings.

Another direct cost to the city was the loss in jobs, income, and tax revenue arising from the closing of 250 businesses that were displaced by the campus and the near West Side urban-renewal prog-

---

[18]Paul Gapp recently pointed out that one cost of the 1962 defeat and thus, indirectly, another social cost of the University decision was Mayor Daley's action to take away the citizens' right to vote on subsequent local bond issues. "Chicago had its tax revolt 16 years ago—and the people lost," *Chicago Tribune,* June 25, 1978, sec. 2, p. 1.

ram. (This would not have happened in the other city locations considered, so it should be considered a cost.) How much the cost was is not estimable without more information as to the character of those businesses. If many were "Mom and Pop" stores rooted in the neighborhood, as I suspect, the cost may have been small in economic terms, although real inasmuch as closing forced the owners into early retirement or to live with other family members. This type of cost would be psychological in nature and thus intangible. If, however, the businesses were large, the economic cost would have been more significant. But I expect that most of the large businesses moved and that over 90 percent of those that moved stayed within the city. If such was the case, the economic costs to the city would be only the cost of moving, since the jobs, the income created, and the tax revenues would remain within the city. This would not be true for the 5–10 percent of the businesses that moved out of the city.

Apart from these broader social costs, the University's presence also has had some direct costs for the neighborhood. The most direct of these is the difficulty residents now have parking in the area, a common cause for complaint. They claim that students park in every available space, including streets, driveways, and even garage space to avoid paying for University parking. At the least this is an annoyance; at the most it may be costly for area residents. Furthermore. residents formerly had parking at least during the evening hours. They now fear that the University's recent initiation of evening classes will seriously worsen the parking problem by excluding residents from parking near their property while classes are in session.

There are no data with respect to crime in this area now as compared with the past. It is known that the entire 12th police district, in which the University area is located, has one of the best crime ratings in the city—second best—and that it has been improving. However, there is some impression among those knowledgeable of the University area that, while other types of crime have fallen, transient crime has increased; much of this is associated with automobile theft, either of a car or of the car's contents. This is not surprising, since over 20,000 transients come into the area almost daily. Criminals can easily mix in, and those living in the neighborhood are no longer able or willing to identify possibly threatening strangers or even to call the police if they see a crime being committed. The campus is also said to have reduced open and institutional space for play and social life in the neighborhood; this may in turn have led to some street-corner activity and petty crime.

Another effect of the campus has been the conflict between neighborhood and student customs. Some of this is the town-and-gown problem associated with all campuses, but it may have been stronger here because of the character of the residents and students. During the early period of the mid-1960s especially, there were sharp issues between Italian landlords and homeowners and the students who rented rooms. It is claimed that students often behaved in a manner that landlords or other residents found bewildering and offensive. Drinking, drug-taking, and informal sex practices of the students ran counter to neighborhood customs. Some residents felt that habits of their family mmbers were being corrupted by the students, and they at times ejected students forcibly. But I am told that this situation has improved markedly as both groups have become more accustomed to each other and as a greater number of serious graduate students have moved into the area.

A general point made by many area residents is that a split exists between the inhabitants of the new developments and the older inhabitants of the neighborhood. The new residents are considered self-contained and withdrawn, bound by inward-looking projects, and not interested in community organizations, the neighborhood, and its people. Those in the developments often regard the older people as formally polite but standoffish and fearful of newcomers. In any case, it is often too much trouble to make an effort to bridge the gap.

The shopping center that has been constructed to serve the area is a frequent cause for complaint. It is believed to have led strangers from outside the area or blacks from the projects along Roosevelt Road to cross through the neighborhood, and both older and newer residents complain of petty thefts and annoyance. But this may be a result of the initial period of change. For example, different groups that shop in the Jewel store have gradually found their own most convenient shopping times, and petty annoyances arising from the mixture have declined.

The direct role of the University campus in the area is very low-key. There is contact at the formal level, and the campus administration responds to complaints. Apart from the administration's making campus recreational facilities available for neighborhood use, there is little real exchange between neighborhood and campus. The University makes little effort to let the people of the neighborhood know what is happening on the campus, and some residents have remarked on this. The housing office is not a particularly useful focal point for helping faculty, staff, and students find accommodations in the area. The University is considered by the neighborhood a silent presence to be respected because it is a major institution of learning, but also one to be feared because of the manner of its entry into the neighborhood and the general ignorance and possible suspicion of its intentions. The University is regarded more as one of the sides of the island created by its construction than as part of that island.

III : *What It All Means*

Economic theory assumes that allocation of resources is *only* through markets and that this assumption holds (implicitly) even if there were [a] mixture of market forms. This view completely overlooks the existence of governments, national and local, where allocations are made not through the medium of markets but by means of voting. . . . [Governments] vote *how much* is to be invested in capital goods, *when* and *where* the investment should take place. . . . Clearly the movement of these funds . . . affects the "free economy" sector of the whole economy with its prices, incomes, allocations.

Oskar Morgenstern, "Thirteen Critical Points in Contemporary Economic Theory: An Interpretation," *Journal of Economic Literature* 10 (1972):1174.

CHAPTER 8

The Choice of Site and
the Approaches to Public Decision-Making

Over the long run, I suspect that what is needed [to better understand and analyze our social problems] may be no less than a radical restructuring of disciplinary boundaries, or at the least, greater tolerance than academia customarily has shown to scholars with interdisciplinary interests.

Richard R. Nelson, *The Moon and the Ghetto* (New York: W. W. Norton, 1977), p. 153.

WHAT LIGHT does the decision to locate the Chicago Circle Campus at its present site throw upon the various approaches to decision-making in the public sector presented in chapter 2? To briefly summarize, four approaches were identified: the first derived from economics centering upon cost-benefit or systems analysis, the second from politics centering on organizational analysis of the governmental unit or units within or among which a decision is made, the third from natural science centering upon a technical approach supposedly above narrower political or economic considerations, and the fourth from sociology and politics stressing the influence of community interest-groups upon decision-makers. Do any of these approaches throw light on this particular decision? In turn, what generalizations can be derived from this decision with respect to these and possibly other approaches that might be tested elsewhere; or is this really a situation of individual "pork-barrels" or bargaining between monoplies, where no generalizations are possible?

If we look first at the relevance of the economic approach, we can summarize by stating that, while economic factors were underlying forces behind the need for a campus, they played a secondary role in the actual choice of a site. Clearly the demand for college education, stimulated first by returning war veterans and later by the postwar baby boom, created a need for the campus in the Chicago area. In addition, the University was influenced by obvious economic factors in its choice of a preferred site: the cost of land, the costs of construction and maintenance of one type of campus as opposed to another, the central location of a campus, and the availability of convenient transportation at reasonable cost to potential students were all important elements in the University's preferences. Similarly, the governor and state legislators were interested in minimizing costs for the campus, since it would be largely financed by the state. Financial costs were also a major constraint for the mayor. But beyond the educational function and the financial burden, the campus had a major potential external economic benefit in the eyes of the mayor: it could contribute to the preservation of Chicago's Loop and central city area.

But although economic and demographic factors underlay the need for another campus, political factors dominated the actual choice of site. The University of Illinois saw its future within a changing state system of public education significantly affected by whether it did or did not construct a Chicago-area campus; it therefore decided to go ahead and construct one. It was also essential that it achieve at least the acquiescence if not support of the city's private universities to a Chicago-area campus if it was to get political support from Chicago's legislators and an influential public opinion. In addition, before the administration could confidently approach legislators for a new campus, it had to convince its own constituency of Champaign-Urbana faculty and officials, as well as the townspeople within the chosen district, that the new campus would not hurt them. For both of these latter goals it was important to prepare a strong technical case, which the University sought to do with its own research and with reports prepared for it by the Real Estate Research Corporation.

The mayor's preference for an inner-city rather than suburban campus was only partly influenced by economic factors. As a resident of Chicago, he had long favored a city campus, and he was also aware that local newspapers, trade unions, businessmen, and civic groups also favored this. Loss of the campus to a suburban location would be a political defeat for him, and he was determined to prevent that. But it was not until after defeat of the proposed Miller Meadows site that University officials recognized his key role in the process, and it may also be that he did not formulate his position until after that had occurred. He had the power to make the choice of a suburban site for the campus very costly to the University, and thus a suburban location would have jeopardized the very gains the University hoped to make from such a campus. Recognition of this meant that the mayor held an effective veto in the negotiations on the site.

The University was able to get a commitment from the mayor that the land for a city campus would cost no more than the same amount of land in the suburbs. Thus the University was relieved of a major economic constraint on locating the campus within Chicago, and it could ask for about the same amount of space it would have had in the suburbs. This in effect shifted the additional economic burden for inner-city space from the University to the city. The mayor in turn sought to shift the burden in two ways. First he attempted to persuade the railroads to give up their yards and stations south of the Loop in exchange for consolidated facilities at the Union and Chicago & North Western Stations and possibly a small payment for their land. The railroads were unwilling to accept this. Then, as the University pressed him in the face of the expected upsurge in enrollments in the ever-nearer future, he finally decided to provide land the city controlled as part of a federal urban-renewal project. This solved two problems: (1) it avoided the need for approval of the necessary action by a local group other than the city, and (2) it enabled the city to get the federal government to take over most of its financing obligation to the University. Thus the economic constraint with respect to cost of inner-city land was lifted from the city, and it could satisfy the University's apparent need for space. While this conversion of land to campus use was made at the expense of a prior commitment to the people of the area, this was regarded as the city's problem. It posed no problem for the University or for the federal and state governments, all of which agreed to accept the city's land-use change, and the courts affirmed the city's right to make that change. The role of the federal government was one of the keys to the decision. Its willingness to provide the subsidy for the land relieved the mayor of the burden of finding the funds to keep his promise to the University. The federal government's willingness to assume this role was not inconsistent with the laws, as the Supreme Court's decision showed. However, it was also assisted by the mayor's close political relationship with the new Democratic president, John F. Kennedy.

The effect of these shifts in financing from University to city to federal government was to deliberately set aside market factors that would have influenced the allocation of land to the University. The external benefits that the city derived from locating the University in the inner city justified the payment of a substantially higher price for the land and property than the University was willing to pay, and two-thirds of this difference in land price was made up by the federal government. The total acquisition cost for the 4.6 million square feet of land and existing property on which the Circle Campus was built was about $27 million (close to $6.0 per square foot); the price at which the land was sold to the University was about $4.6 million (or $1.0 per square foot, which was the same price as an equal amount of suburban land). The city's contribution to this difference in cost was about $7–$8 million; the federal government made up the remainder as a project contribution under the Urban Renewal Law.[1]

The usefulness of a primarily economic approach in explaining this is diminished not only by the bypassing of market constraints on land costs. It is in fact when market prices are considered to be an unsatisfactory measure of social costs and benefits that the use of shadow prices representing "social" values is recommended to achieve correct benefit/cost results. But in this case there are very serious problems in measuring the external economic benefits of placing the University in one location as compared with another. The attempt to indicate benefits and costs in the previous chapter has shown some of these problems.

One problem that is obvious is the difficulty of measurement. What are the supposed benefits of stabilizing the near West Side as compared with those of possibly stablizing the Garfield Park area or compared with what might have occurred by the development already underway on the near West Side? How does one measure the costs of uprooting a large part of a neighborhood (and what are the probabilities that it might have been uprooted anyway)? Apart from these economic benefits, which are at least conceptually if not practically

---

[1] These figures, which are from government files on the three projects that subsequently made up the University site, are approximate for various reasons. There were differences in the raw data over time. Also, only 51 percent of the land acquired as the Congress-Racine project was for the campus, and I have crudely prorated project costs accordingly. The city's contribution varied from one-fourth to one-third of the total costs for each project, depending upon the project's date, since the law that covered sharing between city and federal government on an urban renewal project changed during this period.

measurable, how does one measure the political cost to the city's inhabitants of reversing, in what must seem an arbitrary fashion, decisions and plans that had been democratically arrived at? How does one measure the political costs and benefits of choosing one location as opposed to another, which must have been a major consideration in the thinking not only of Mayor Daley but also of such state legislators as Senator Peters and which clearly entered the thinking of the University's representatives when they had to decide whether or not to go to the state legislature over Miller Meadows?

The deliberate replacement of the market as a device to allocate land by nonmarket factors would make any measure of optimality difficult. The nonmeasurability of the major external benefits and costs of the decision, whether economic or political, and the inevitable disagreement over weights to be given to the various benefits or costs make it impossible to determine in any remotely precise fashion the optimality of the decision reached or, even more important, which among the sites considered was optimal.

But, apart from the difficulties of measurement or of weighting alternative objectives, the cost-benefit approach has more basic weaknesses that arise from the nature of the decision-making process I have already indicated at the start of the previous chapter. The only times when there was any real possibility of carefully appraising each of the alternatives was in 1955, at the very start of the University's search for a site, and again, but less so, in 1958. In 1955 the Real Estate Research Corporation and the University agreed on a set of criteria; they examined 69 sites on the basis of these criteria and selected Miller Meadows and an island in Lake Michigan as preferred. When Miller Meadows proved unavailable, the search procedure was repeated in 1958; from among 78 possible sites four preferred locations were selected, each of which already had substantial public backing. But, because of the loss of time in the intervening period, the weighting of advantages had changed.

None of the four sites preferred in 1958 proved available or acceptable, and a seventh site never preferred in *any* previous selection process was identified and chosen. The site had not previously been considered available; but the previous reports had not considered, and probably could not consider, many of the key intangible elements, such as the effects of a location on racial balance or its political costs and benefits. As a consequence, these reports served more as a public relations effort and less as a guide for the decision-makers. They served to confirm locations that either the city or the University already preferred rather than to weigh the real advantages and disadvantages of a site as perceived by the decision-makers.

Then, after 1957 and failure of the effort to get Miller Meadows, the decision-makers, whether University or city, did not really have the luxury of choice among alternatives; rather, the choices came in sequence. When Miller Meadows proved unavailable, the University next desired Riverside Golf Club. But that choice was unrealistic and was withdrawn by the University when the mayor offered to contribute funds for a city site. The mayor then suggested the railroad yards, which were unavailable, and the other sites suggested in the 1958 report proved unacceptable to the city. While this was going on, the benefits and costs of the sites were changing, simply because time was passing. Consequently, University officials perceived that potential students were coming closer to becoming actual students, and that should a campus not be made available for them quickly in Chicago they would have to be educated elsewhere—a move that would lessen the need for a University of Illinois campus in Chicago and reduce the benefits to be derived from it. The mayor, meanwhile, risked loss of the campus entirely if he could not come up with the required land. Thus an area considered undesirable and unavailable at the start of the search and ruled out in 1958 as an urban-renewal residental project became not only available but "the only game in town" when, as pointed out, the search was confronted with an all-or-none decision. An economic approach using a cost-benefit analysis would not have predicted this outcome at the start of what turned out to be a sequential process rather than a process of optimizing among alternatives; neither was the approach necessary at the end, when there really was no alternative.

What is regrettable is that market forces were not given greater recognition in the decision. If either the University or the city had to pay all or a greater portion of the higher price of inner-city land rather than being able to shift the balance to the federal government, the result might have been a different, possibly smaller, campus that would not have altered the chosen neighborhood (or some other) as drastically as it did; or if the city had had to pay the higher price anyway, it might have been willing to offer more to the railroads for the land in the railroad yards. But the heavy subsidy paid by the federal government to the city for the campus land as an urban-renewal project made consideration of either of these alternatives unnecessary.

This experience might warrant consideration by the federal government of some type of legislation that would permit a federal subsidy for the purchase of land on the condition that such purchase would lead to the preservation of a neighborhood by constructing public buildings in an open rather than an occupied residential area. For example, a subsidy amounting to all or part of the cost of buying an occupied piece of ground might be used instead to buy an unoccupied plot of land for public buildings when the use of the occupied plot for such buildings would destroy a neighborhood. Such a subsidy might have the effect of saving a neighborhood. If a subsidy of that type had been available to the city, it might have been used to buy the railroad yards in time to meet the deadline for the University's needs. There is general agreement that the yards would have been a better choice for the campus in terms of the mayor's goals, and their external costs would have been far lower, since they were largely unoccupied. However, they were simply not available at the price the city was willing to pay in any feasible time period; and they remain underutilized and are still being discussed as a possible location for a variety of public or private uses.

As Nelson points out, there are similarities between the economic approach and the technical approach toward decision-making; the differences are more in who is to do the decision-making, whether economists or scientists. The University laid a good deal of stress upon the quality of its technical analysis and its prestige as the best public institution of higher education in the state. The various internal committees that were set up carried out technical analyses that developed a need for the campus, identified a preferred type of campus, estimated the space required for that type of campus, and explored the relation between program needs and the use of space as well as other issues. In addition, once the type of campus and space were determined, the University asked the Real Estate Research Corporation to carry out a technical analysis to determine the appropriate site and

Skidmore, Owings & Merrill to lay out tentative plans for a campus at each site.

Among the most important of these in their consequences for the choice of a site were the space studies. Both the analysis of costs of construction and maintenance and the examination of other urban campuses led to a conclusion that a low-rise campus of discrete buildings was the preferred type. This was consistent with a strong belief among University officials that such a campus created a better academic and social environment for students and faculty than any other type. This was a major factor in justifying the University's need for space, which remained a more or less fixed element in the entire process and in the early stage of the search helped to explain the University's preference for a campus in the suburbs. The quality of the technical analysis, supported by the University's prestige as an educational institution, made it possible for the University to insist on and get what it considered to be adequate space, even in the inner city.

The University's technical prestige in the state and its large number of graduates gave it a good deal of political weight in the legislature and with the governor as well as with the mayor. Its awareness of this prestige, joined with its political influence, may have caused it, when it sought Miller Meadows, to overestimate its political strength in the conflict with the Forest Preserve District. But even after the loss of that site, the weight of its prestige was significant in convincing the mayor not only that Chicago should have a University of Illinois campus within its boundaries, but also that it was the best judge of its own space requirements for a high quality education. Furthermore, its prestige and technical competence were undoubtedly significant factors in eventually persuading the private universities in the city to accept as inevitable (although with varying degrees of reluctance) the construction of a city campus. The same aura helped to persuade at least some residents of the Harrison-Halsted area that location of the University there would be an advantage worth the admittedly heavy cost. It unquestionably played an even larger role in persuading influential members of the city and state establishments as well as the newspapers, to accept the final location. This element of technical prestige that some educational and scientific institutions have is an important part of their strength against competing institutions or policies that might operate against them.[2]

But the organizational approach goes still further in explaining the character of this decision-making process. At least part of the University's interest in a Chicago campus arose from its desire to safeguard its present strong position in the state's educational system for the future. Many of the difficulties with respect to a choice of site rose directly from the complexity of the governmental system. Such semi-independent government agencies as the Forest Preserve District, the Cook County Board, and the Park District had sufficient strength to oppose the University; and Mayor Daley could have used their opposition for his own ends or he may have decided he could not counter them at that time. The opposition of those agencies was sufficiently strong to prevent location of the campus in Miller Meadows and may well have been a significant factor in the mayor's reluctance to support Garfield Park or Northerly Island as feasible sites. Finally, the peculiar legal rights of the railroads under state law made it possible for them to prevent the city from condemning their yards and terminals for use as a campus.

But the effects of the organizational system were not all negative. Pressure from Chicago legislators in the state legislature contributed to a decision to build a permanent campus in the Chicago area. It was from within the city's urban-renewal administration that the suggestion of the final site surfaced to the mayor; and it was the promise made to the University of this city government's strong support of the Harrison-Halsted site that played a significant part in the University's decision to accept it. In my opinion, this experience with respect to location of the Chicago Circle Campus supports Nelson's emphasis on the importance of organizational factors within the government in decision-making. However, it casts some doubt on Nelson's conclusion that this approach is a better aid in explaining a decision already made than a guide in making a better decision. If one considers an inner-city site as preferable to a suburban site, as I do, then it was the mayor's insistence on the former, based upon his own experience and goals for the city as well as upon the political benefits he would derive

---

[2]Theodore J. Lowi and Benjamin Ginsberg, *Poliscide* (New York: Macmillan, 1976), stress this.

from such a choice, that led to the selection of the better site in that respect.

Finally, what does the community-influence approach contribute to the choice of the site or to an explanation of the decision process? What is clear is that many communities were involved and had an effect upon both the University and city's decisions. With respect to the University, public pressure from the students and faculty at Navy Pier as expressed in meetings with University officials and board members played some role in convincing the Board of Trustees that they must seriously consider setting up a campus in Cook County. Representative Randolph, who had the strong support of Chicago newspapers, trade unions, Pier students and their parents, and the Garfield Park community, by his legislative actions influenced the decision of the University to build a Cook County campus. Opposition to such a location from some of the private universities led to the need to reconcile those institutions by means of adjustments in the proposed educational program for the campus and thus contributed somewhat to the shape of the program that was eventually worked out for the campus's first decade. The University's need to satisfy its Urbana constituency was also a significant factor in the decision that evolved. But while these community groups played an important role in the University's decision to go ahead with the campus, their role in making the decision concerning a specific location within the city was not as significant.

Important business, labor, and ethnic groups in Chicago, as well as the city's newspapers, strongly opposed a suburban site and favored a city location. They played a role, though not a very important one on the surface, in the Miller Meadows struggle. Their role in the failure of the University's short-lived effort to acquire Riverside Golf Club was probably more obvious. Once a suburban site was eliminated, however, many of these groups played a less important role in the selection of the specific location of the campus within the city. In this respect, probably the major influence upon the mayor was the State Street Council, which represents leading Loop businesses, banks, and real estate firms.

The State Street Council strongly supported a campus in the South Loop railroad yards and Terminal site to serve as an anchor for the Loop. But this position was not a united business effort; the obvious exceptions were the railroads themselves, which neither favored consolidation of the terminals nor consented to give up the required acreage in the years and terminals without greater payment than the city was willing to offer. Their reluctance to do this led to the failure of that plan. (One railway was supposedly prepared to give up its terminal area of about 30 acres as a gift to the University, but this space was considered so small that the offer was never formalized.[3])

The business groups also opposed the use of Northerly Island for the campus, and this contributed to the mayor's opposition to that location. Perhaps most important, those groups, together with the broader Joint Action Committee, strongly opposed the Garfield Park site, which was also opposed by conservation groups and probably the Park District. This opposition certainly played a part in the mayor's unwillingness to publicly support Garfield Park, in spite of the strong support that site had from white community groups in the area, which sought to limit the entry of blacks there, and from such a large business firm as Sears, Roebuck, which had its headquarters nearby.

The mayor's preferences and action were not determined by a united business group. The failure of the railroad-yard plan indicates that there was no such group. The mayor himself placed great weight upon the preservation and strengthening of the Loop as a center of business. His preference was consistent with but was not dominated by that of many of the city's leading business firms and banks, for whom the life of the Loop was of crucial importance, even though their support had become a major element in his political strength.

Thus, when the Terminal site collapsed as a viable alternative within the ever-tightening time limitation, the mayor bypassed Garfield Park, which was four miles from the Loop and was opposed by business and conservation groups as well as the city's own Park District, to select the Harrison-Halsted site. The latter was located near enough to the Loop to satisfy the business groups that had supported the railroad yards. It was already under the city's control, so the organization problems that had plagued earlier choices would be minimized. It was also eligible for substantial federal funding that

---

[3]Interview with Charles Genther of the UICC faculty, March 9, 1978, Author's Papers.

could be used to meet the mayor's financial commitment to the University. However, the selection of the Harrison-Halsted site required that the mayor disregard previous commitments made to residents of the area and modify the already-passed City Council ordinances that embodied those commitments. But by this time he had little choice if he wished to have the campus in the city at all. There was pressure from both the University's needs and his own political plans for the next election.

The mayor checked the choice with the 1st Ward committeeman, who reluctantly agreed to it; and the mayor then moved ahead. He anticipated some opposition but not opposition led by neighborhood women which, in addition, was probably heavier than he expected. But, while this opposition was vocal and embarrassing, it was not decisive. It had no support from major elements of the Chicago establishment, and it had no funds with which to harass him in the long run. In addition, the neighborhood was not united in its opposition. The residents who were not displaced generally went along with the city, either because they had city jobs or because they felt they had no other choice. While this opposition may have cost the mayor the 1962 bond issue, it had little or no effect on the far more important 1963 election.

The mayor in effect sacrificed the interests of part of a neighborhood for other aims that he himself and powerful supporters considered more important than what was lost in the sacrificed community. Among the aims he abandoned was what he expressed about neighborhoods in his inaugural remarks when he said, "Chicago is a city of neighborhoods and I resolve to be mayor of all the neighborhoods. . . ."[4] But the decision reached was not inconsistent with the best technical thinking on urban development at the time, which stressed large redevelopment with massive slum clearance rather than neighborhood preservation. Chicago had had many previous examples of such large slum-clearance redevelopment projects, as also had New York City under the influence of Robert Moses. While the importance of neighborhood preservation was beginning to be recog-

[4]Eugene Kennedy, *Himself! The Life and Times of Richard J. Daley* (New York: Viking Press, 1978), p. 133.

nized, it was not until Jane Jacobs's *The Death and Life of Great American Cities*[5] in 1961 that there was a sharp turn in thinking to favor that policy as a key to urban revival. This did not change policy until even later, and by that time it was far too late for the Harrison-Halsted area.

To summarize this phase of the discussion, this experience does not support those theories of decision-making that postulate a united business community dominating a city government. The business community was not united and the mayor was not weak. But it does support a picture of an important role for community influence groups; of conflict over the use of land; and of a willingness to sacrifice a weaker community group, in this case the Italian, Greek, and Spanish-speaking peoples of the near West Side, for the interests of stronger groups, in this case the University and the Loop business community. This sacrifice had in its support the prestige of the University, the technical expertise of the city planner, and the long-standing desire for a University of Illinois campus in Chicago.

This experience may also support Hirschman's theory of a "hiding hand" in project planning, although, if so, it was more by chance than by any systematic tendency I can determine. The previous chapter argues that the choice turned out well for the University, that the site was probably better than any other seriously considered and available, and that it certainly was better than a suburban site.[6] It did not turn out poorly for the neighborhood or the city, although it is not possible to compare the results achieved with what they would have been under the neighborhood's own plans. It apparently has achieved a desired stabilization of the area by turning it into an island. There was a real loss, however, in terms of the cost of people moving out of the area and in the effect the manner in which the decision was made had upon democratic planning in the city. Whether that stabilization is a benefit or a cost depends upon whether the plans for the neighborhood that existed would have turned it into a prosperous, integrated

[5](New York: Vintage Books, 1961), ch. 15 especially. D. Bowly, Jr., *The Poor House* (Carbondale: Southern Illinois University Press, 1978), describes the period of public housing construction in Chicago in the 1960s as the "high-rise years." See ch. 7, especially pp. 111–12 and 127–28.

[6]This, in hindsight, is also Charles Havens's position today; although at that time he considered Northerly Island (Meigs Field) the best site.

area as was hoped when the area's plans were developed or whether the area would have become like the district south of Roosevelt Road as city officials and others feared. In any event, it is not a quantifiable benefit. But if the net balance of the decision has been positive, as I believe, it was not anticipated at the start of the decision process, and it depended greatly upon the city's willingness to spend heavily in the neighborhood both to fulfill commitments to the University and to calm resident opposition.

Selection of this site was the result of a sudden and unpremeditated choice, and there was no reason, from the decision process itself, for a favorable outcome. In fact, the experience tends to support Lowi's skeptical view of the values of pluralism, in contrast with Banfield's more favorable view, as previously discussed in chapter 2. While this location decision was under consideration for a long time, the actual site selected was never considered as an alternative until *after* the city had informally made its decision. At that time there was little chance for any discusssion to influence the choice of that site. The ends sacrificed by the manner of making this decision are those inherent in the practice of democratic, up-from-the-bottom community planning for a neighborhood as opposed to central decision-making from the top and those ends that might have been achieved by retaining a neighborhood rather than clearing a substantial part of it. The failure of the opposition to gain widespread public support against the decision and the mayor's re-election in spite of it may indicate that Chicago supported the sacrifice of those ends for the presence of the University.

Finally, this study has thrown light on Yates's characterization of Mayor Daley in Chicago and on the governance of cities in general. If this decision is an example of the former mayor's style, Yates has described him in far too passive terms. The mayor played a major role, much of it behind the scenes, in bringing the campus to downtown Chicago rather than to the suburbs. While the final site selection was not his first choice and represented a compromise in the face of opposition to other preferred sites, he took responsibility and, knowingly, also the political heat for that selection as the final choice. The result was a campus in Chicago that many of the city's inhabitants had long wanted. This is an example of the mayor's leadership rather than passivity as Yates describd it. But, while this conclusion casts doubt on Yates's picture of Mayor Daley's role in Chicago and on his general conclusions as they apply to this type of decision, it does not disprove his overall conclusion concerning the ungovernability of cities. Site selection of campuses may have been one of those types of decision that Yates argues are becoming rarer—a type that can still be made clearly and over which a mayor can still exercise strong leadership. It would be interesting, however, to explore, by means of further research into how such site decisions have been made in cities other than Chicago, whether this is in fact the case and also to compare decision-making in such cases with decision-making in other fields.

Other states, cities, and even countries have gone through selection processes for other universities or scientific installations in recent years. Many new campuses were constructed in cities in the late 1950s and 1960s. Some obvious examples are the Albany campus in New York, the Milwaukee campus in Wisconsin, the San Diego campus in California, and the San Antonio campus in Texas, to name a few. In Illinois itself other new state universities were built in Springfield and in the Chicago suburbs. To go farther afield, England saw a great construction of "red brick" universities in its cities and new campuses were also built in major cities of many other European countries. In India the new Jawaharlal Nehru University was built outside Delhi. How were these location decisions made?

If we were to establish a system of decision-making relationships based upon the Chicago Circle Campus in Illinois, it would stress the relationship between a major state university, with the prestige of its technical reputation and its access to technical expertise, and the rest of the state's public higher-education system and the state government, the governor and the legislature, the mayor of the city concerned, and the numerous quasi-independent legal bodies that own land in or near the city. These in turn were strongly influenced but not controlled in their approach to the issue of location by pressures from interested community groups. In addition, the federal government played an important supporting role by supplying funds; but it did not have an independent role. Economic determinants of choice were subordinated to political determinants, both from the very nature of the goals of the major parties involved, and from the institutional setting, by the manner in which price incentives that might have operated for or against the choice of a location were bypassed; instead of price, time and space were the major constraints in this decision. The interests of students as consumers were strongly recognized in the criteria of choice used; but the interests of the neighborhood in which the campus was to be set were considered of only minor importance.

Would there be a similar process in other states where the position of the state university is different both in its relationship with other parts of the public-education system and in relation to the state? (The California and New York systems are significantly different from the Illinois system, and the technical prestige of the separate institutions in those systems varies greatly from one to the other and from the position of the Urbana campus in Illinois.) What difference did the power of the governor make—for example, Rockefeller in New York —in contrast with the power of a city leader such as Daley? What powers did the city or state have with respect to condemnation of land? Did the organizational complexity of the local governments in those states make a difference in the result, and what was the relationship of the local governments and political leaders to the state government? How did community pressure groups influence or seek to influence the decision? Did economic factors, such as market price of land, play a significant role in the location decision? How did those factors influence the decision, or were they bypassed? What was the part, if any, played by the federal government? How was the campus related to the neighborhood in which it was constructed, and what part did neighborhood objections or demands play in the choice? What were the other desired external benefits and costs of the location and how important were these? What, in fact, were the effects of the location; for example, did it preserve a neighborhood, protect an area from deterioration, conserve an environment, or have yet other consequences?

In the European and Asian countries that are not federal in political structure or in which the central government plays a direct educational role, did the processes and results differ significantly? Do the economic and technical factors play a greater role in such countries than in the United States, since the central government can act in terms of a national rather than local interest? What is the relationship between the central decision-makers and the university administration, the local interest group, and the neighborhood? Do stated goals

change, and what about the actual results? Does the national decision-making process simplify the decision process, or does it compli-
cate the process by introducing numerous national considerations
into the issue?

So far I have discussed this issue in terms of the location of an
educational institution. But similar considerations may enter into
other types of locational decision-making. In Chicago the issue of
construction and location of a new sports stadium, as reported in the
newspapers, bears marked similarities to the matter of the campus, at
least on superficial examination; and in still another field, the decision-making related to the now discarded plan for construction and
location of the Crosstown Expressway seemed bounded by a similar
group of variables and constraints. The capital improvement budget
for the city of Chicago for the period 1974–78 totaled $7.5 billion, of
which the city contributed $2.3 billion and other governmental units
the remainder. This included the construction of over 1,000 public
projects in Chicago. During fiscal year 1976 the Illinois Capital
Development Board had an appropriation of over $800 million to
spend for more than 1,000 capital improvements in the state.[7] Many
of these city and state projects will require significant location decisions by one or more levels of the government, and the issues they
will raise may be comparable or similar to those raised in the campus-
site decision. This type of decision-making is certainly an important
sector of the economy that is deserving of further analysis both to
further understanding of how decisions are made and, possibly, to
improve the decision results from society's point of view.

Robert Caro[8] has examined the decision-making process on public-sector projects in New York State when Robert Moses was the
major decision-maker. The issues there, and the results, were similar
to those in Chicago and other large cities at about the same time.
Further comparison of such decision-making among major cities
may lead to significant insights into the process. How important were
the Moseses, the Daleys, and the other individuals in the decision-

[7]Department of Development and Planning, *1974–1978 Improvements Program* (Chicago:
City of Chicago, 1974), p. vi; and *An Accountability Budget for Illinois Fiscal Year 1977*
(Springfield: State of Illinois, 1976), p. 260. Fiscal year 1977 extended from July 1, 1976, to
June 30, 1977.

[8]*The Power Broker* (New York: Vintage Books, 1975).

making, and what effect did their different political strengths, weaknesses, and styles and the different organizational frameworks within which they functioned have upon the results? Do different methods of project analysis, with different weights given to economic and technical factors, yield different project results? Are general factors the determinants in the types of decision made, or are the key individuals the determinants? In reading about the proposed Westway Project in New York, I find that the technical, economic, and social issues and difficulties are not unlike those involved in the decision-making process for the Crosstown Expressway in Chicago. As neighborhood groups in recent years have sought to play a larger role in location decisions that affect them, comparisons have become noticeable in the aims of such groups and their effects on decision-making. Robert Werner has written an interesting paper about the effect a community group has had upon the plans of New York City to build a sewage disposal plant on the Hudson River.[9] Werner's description of community action in New York resembles that of the Harrison-Halsted Community Group at the campus site, but it was more successful. Such efforts raise questions concerning the appropriate role of a neighborhood community in site decision-making, the relationship between neighborhood and city, and the meaning of democracy in such conflict situations.

I think comparative studies of public-sector urban decision-making for locations can yield fruitful results. The present study with respect to general principles of urban decision-making has been an attempt to identify key actors, major elements in their thinking, and possible relationships among the actors and their goals. Whether it is possible to develop a more precise theory with stronger interrelationships that can predict specific results given certain known relationships or that can go farther and identify a best location is doubtful, but further comparative analysis using the identified variables may throw light on the probabilities of a given choice. As an economist, I find that one regrettable conclusion of this study is the relatively minor role played by economic analysis in this decision; another is the weakness of a cost/benefit approach, based on economics, as a guide

[9]R. Werner, "Siting a Sewage Treatment Plant on the Hudson" (term paper submitted at Columbia University, New York, 1975).

for the decision-maker. I would like to add that a framework of decision-making that would permit economic factors to play a greater role in the process would be desirable by setting some objective limits within which decision-makers may better act. While it is probably inevitable that in public-sector decisions of this type political factors will dominate, a greater role granted to such objective considerations as price might improve the results for those affected.

Appendix A

CONCURRENT CALENDAR OF MAJOR EVENTS IN THE
DECISION TO LOCATE THE CHICAGO CIRCLE CAMPUS AT
HARRISON-HALSTED

YEAR	UNIVERSITY OF ILLINOIS	STATE OF ILLINOIS, STATE ELECTIONS
Late 1930s		
1941		
1945		Sen. Daley introduces bill for University branch in Chicago
1946	Navy Pier branch approved and started, funds requested from legislature	
1947		Legislature passes budget for Pier campus
1948		
1949		
1950		

CITY OF CHICAGO, COOK COUNTY	HARRISON-HALSTED RESIDENTS, HULL-HOUSE	JOINT ACTION COMMITTEE, OTHER PRIVATE INTERESTED GROUPS
	Jane Addams Public Housing Project built	
	Medical Center District established	
Leases Navy Pier to University		
	West Side Community Committee set up to consider future of area; meets with Hull-House to discuss what to do	
	Temporary Organizing Committee (TOC) set up	
	Aug.: Hulbert appointed as consultant to TOC	
	West Side Community Committee work continues	
	June: TOC converted into Near West Side Planning Board (NWPB)	
Pistilli Ordinance passed	Conflict over Pistilli Ordinance, resolved in acceptable fashion	
	NWPB develops support for idea of planning; does research on character of area; mobilizes residents for development of area rehabilitation program; discusses area's future with city officials and agencies	

YEAR	UNIVERSITY OF ILLINOIS	STATE OF ILLINOIS, STATE ELECTIONS
1951		
1952	Stoddard reports on need for Chicago campus, mentions possible location north of Medical Center	
1953	*May, June:* Navy Pier faculty and students meet with Stoddard and Board of Trustees (BOT) to request 4-year Pier program	
	July 24: Stoddard resigns	
	July 25: Committee, established by BOT for issue, reports	
	Morey appointed acting president	
	Morey appoints Committee on Future Development of Chicago Undergraduate Division (Louthitt Committee) to consider Chicago-area campus, as counterpart to Randolph Committee	Randolph Committee set up to report to state legislature on establishment of 4-year campus in Chicago area
1954	*April:* Interim report of Committee on Future Development (CFD)	
	Board approves first contract with Real Estate Research Corporation (RERC) to report to CFD	
	July: Final report of CFD	
	Board approves contract with RERC to recommend site	
	Caveny Committee reports on building types and land use for campus	

CITY OF CHICAGO, COOK COUNTY	HARRISON-HALSTED RESIDENTS, HULL-HOUSE	JOINT ACTION COMMITTEE, OTHER PRIVATE INTERESTED GROUPS
Designates 55-acre tract east of Halsted for industrial use		
Requests part of Pier back; withdraws request	NWPB work continues	
	NWPB work continues	
	NWPB work continues	

YEAR	UNIVERSITY OF ILLINOIS	STATE OF ILLINOIS, STATE ELECTIONS
1955	*Feb.:* Report by RERC recommending island in Lake Michigan and Miller Meadows; CFD recommends reverse	Randolph Committee reports in favor of Chicago-area campus with 4-year program
	Informal soundings begun with Forest Preserve District, state, and city on Miller Meadows	Rep. Randolph introduces bill for $4 million for campus with 4-year program in Chicago area, without specific site; Sen. Pollack introduces bill for $5 million for campus at Riverview Park; University opposes both bills; both defeated
	Discussions with Illinois Institute of Technology (IIT) concerning campus nearby	
	Continued correspondence and meetings between Morey and presidents of city's private institutions	
	U. of I. Alumni Association favors suburban Chicago campus	
	Henry selected as president; visits Chicago in June, takes office in September	
1956	Further studies for site preparation; comparative studies of other urban universities on site characteristics	University requests $2 million in 1957-59 budget for land acquisition and site studies for Miller Meadows
	June: BOT votes to start process for acquiring Miller Meadows	Illinois Higher Education Commission opposes 4-year campus and opposes night school or residence halls

CITY OF CHICAGO, COOK COUNTY	HARRISON-HALSTED RESIDENTS, HULL-HOUSE	JOINT ACTION COMMITTEE, OTHER PRIVATE INTERESTED GROUPS
April: Daley elected mayor; Johnston discusses Miller Meadows site with him	Schwartzhaupt Foundation grants Hull-House $40,000 for community organization work in area to be funneled through NWPB *May:* Hulbert dies Giovangelo becomes acting director; executive committee of NWPB recommends he be appointed director; Hull-House refuses, begins separate Community Participation Project using Schwartzhaupt Fund grant	
Opposition to choice of Miller Meadows by Forest Preserve District board, by board's advisory committee, and by Cook County board of commissioners	Three city council ordinances passed concerning near West Side area; two of the three legalized a 240-acre conservancy area west of Harrison-Halsted and a 55-acre clearance area at Harrison-Halsted for residential use	

YEAR	UNIVERSITY OF ILLINOIS	STATE OF ILLINOIS, STATE ELECTIONS
1957	University decides not to seek state legislation for Miller Meadows BOT opposes state site legislation University begins to consider alternative sites to Miller Meadows; Henry convinced of Daley's key role, in September writes to mayor on matter	Legislature allocates $950,000 for new campus Rep. Randolph introduces bill for Chicago campus; bill introduced in senate for Cook County campus with programs similar to Urbana; both defeated Legislature passes bill authorizing $248 million bond issue, including $35 million for permanent Chicago-area campus, to come up in 1958 elections Sen. Peters favors downtown site
1958	*March:* BOT requests another study by RERC to select a site, asks for detailed studies of Riverside Golf Club and Terminal site Low morale of Navy Pier administration, faculty, and staff *Oct.:* RERC report suggests four sites, excluding urban clearance areas	*Nov.:* Proposed bond issue defeated Three Republican members of BOT defeated; Democratic board after March 1959

CITY OF CHICAGO, COOK COUNTY	HARRISON-HALSTED RESIDENTS, HULL-HOUSE	JOINT ACTION COMMITTEE, OTHER PRIVATE INTERESTED GROUPS
Forest Preserve District sponsors a study by DeLeeuw, Cather & Co.; study opposes Miller Meadows, suggests near West Side site north of Medical Center Mayor nominates Bach to work with University on site location; discussions start on Rail Terminal site	NWPB ended; local resident groups begin planning Citizens Participation Project under Hull-House auspices to meet with local businessmen; discussion of international shopping center begun; city officials meet with local business and resident groups Near West Side Conservation Commission council set up after hearings with city and federal government officials to develop program for area	*April:* Garfield Park–Austin Community Council urges Garfield Park site *May:* Chicago Central Area Committee discusses site with University; favors one of three inner-city sites, including Rail Terminal south of Loop *June: Chicago Tribune* opposes Miller Meadows, favors site in or near Loop *Nov.: Daily News* reports Miller Meadows definitely out
Aug.: Central Area Plan for Chicago published; Terminal area designated for campus, Harrison-Halsted area for residential development	Haring hired to develop plan for area; city council approves plan for Harrison-Halsted area for residential and limited commercial use; contract is signed with federal government; Land Clearance Commission begins acquiring and clearing plots of land in area; Holy Guardian Angel Church buys land for school	

YEAR	UNIVERSITY OF ILLINOIS	STATE OF ILLINOIS, STATE ELECTIONS

1959

University of Illinois

Feb.: BOT votes in favor of Riverside Golf Club and Northerly Island as preferred sites, urges action be started to acquire the former

University accepts Daley's request and offer

May 16: New BOT favors Garfield Park as site, urges action to transfer land to University

July: Henry writes presidents of private Chicago universities concerning night school programs

Skidmore, Owings & Merrill conducts planning studies for campus at alternative sites throughout year

University agrees with Park District and city to begin legal testing of issues arising from Garfield Park land transfer

BOT considers Garfield Park only feasible site

Students at Pier demonstrate in mayor's office to urge site action

State of Illinois, State Elections

April: Gov. Stratton proposes new bond issue

House of Representatives opposes suburban site

June: State legislature votes $195 million bond issue bill for state universities, including $50 million for new Chicago campus of U. of I. and $25 million for Edwardsville campus of SIU

Legislature appropriates $2.5 million in new funds for land purchase and planning and site preparation for new campus

Legislature passes bill making possible transfer of land from Park District to University

Dec.: Legislative Committee to Visit State Institutions finds acute emergency at Navy Pier

CITY OF CHICAGO, COOK COUNTY	HARRISON-HALSTED RESIDENTS, HULL-HOUSE	JOINT ACTION COMMITTEE, OTHER PRIVATE INTERESTED GROUPS
Feb. 23: Daley asks University to defer selection of Golf Club, offers to defray extraordinary costs of land arising from selection of city instead of suburban site	Holy Guardian Angel School is built and dedicated	Strong protests both in Riverside and in city against Golf Club site
May: Daley re-elected mayor	Harrison-Halsted Residents and Businessmen's Association incorporated, to support redevelopment plan for area, to serve as purchaser of plots of land for residential renewal	Garfield Park groups meet with Henry and Daley to urge site
May 6: Daley asks University to consider Terminal site as first choice and Garfield Park as alternative		*Garfieldian* and other private groups in Garfield Park favor Garfield Park site; president of Sears, Roebuck writes mayor favoring that site; much action on this throughout year
May 15: city rejects Meigs Field site	*Dec.:* Downs of Hull-House BOT favors Hull-House sponsored co-op housing program in Harrison-Halsted area	
Agreement on procedure to test legal status of Garfield Park land transfer to University		*May:* Joint Action Committee of Civic Organizations (JAC) set up to support Terminal site and oppose Garfield Park
Dec.: Daley separates issue of terminal consolidation and site selection		
City officials decide secretly to consider Harrison-Halsted possible alternative campus site		

1960

March: BOT approves proposal to city and Park District to acquire Garfield Park

June: Henry states Garfield Park to be University choice

Aug.: Havens informs internal University committee of likelihood of offer of Harrison-Halsted, and that city favors it

Sept. 14, 20: Havens alerts BOT to forthcoming site offer, and problems of area

Studies Harrison-Halsted site, asks Skidmore, Owings & Merrill to do engineering studies and site plans

Carries out major campaign for proposed bond issue started in 1959, accelerating in 1960

Dec.: Henry appoints Parker vice-president of Chicago campus

Henry dubious of new site until Skidmore, Owings & Merrill present plans to deal satisfactorily with underground utility lines

Nov.: Bond issue with funds for Circle Campus wins election; Kerner and Kennedy elected governor and president

CITY OF CHICAGO, COOK COUNTY	HARRISON-HALSTED RESIDENTS, HULL-HOUSE	JOINT ACTION COMMITTEE, OTHER PRIVATE INTERESTED GROUPS
Jan.: City policy scandal	*April 28:* Downs informs Hull-House BOT of possibility of Harrison-Halsted area as alternative site	JAC enters Garfield Park case to prevent sale of land
April: Legal action to test legality of 1959 state legislation concerning Garfield Park		*May 11: Daily News* prints in one edition only story that Harrison-Halsted is considered an alternate site
Discussions between railroads and city on Terminal site clearly at impasse	*May 26:* Downs reports again	
	Movement by residents proceeds to implement area-development plan; discussions carried on with possibly interested developers	*July 6: Sun-Times* discusses Harrison-Halsted as possible site
May 1: Daley asks department of city planning to prepare plan for campus at Harrison-Halsted; University informed of plans but not of location		*Dec.: Tribune* favors Garfield Park at Henry's request
June 21: University informed that Harrison-Halsted is area considered	Downs in summer meeting of Hull-House BOT tells of likely offer in near future and of expected sequence of events	
Aug. 26: Cook County Judge Harrington rules 1959 legislation unconstitutional	*Sept. 29:* Downs informs Hull-House BOT of formal offer, anticipates action, but stresses lack of definiteness until University accepts site, urges Hull-House to take no public position on matter until it becomes more definite	
Sept. 27: Daley and city officials formally offer Harrison-Halsted site to University		
Oct. 6: Chicago Plan Commission formally changes Central Area Plan for Chicago to shift campus location from Terminal site to Harrison-Halsted	Isolated protests against campus location	

YEAR	UNIVERSITY OF ILLINOIS	STATE OF ILLINOIS, STATE ELECTIONS
1961	Queries Park District on latter's willingness to sell Garfield Park area for campus site; Harrison-Halsted site compared with Garfield Park; crucial issues are site availability and city support *Feb. 10:* BOT meets with Daley *Feb. 15:* BOT accepts Harrison-Halsted site offer *Feb. 17:* Henry informs Daley *June:* Henry announces plans for Hull-House	State Supreme Court overrules Harrington decision *June:* Legislature passes University budget, including $4.6 million for purchase of Harrison-Halsted site *Aug.:* State law permitting use of redevelopment land for building schools and for city to set up department of urban renewal State housing board approves areas for project
1962	BOT approves contract with city for land purchase at $1.008 per square foot, but construction delayed by suits	Federal Housing and Home Finance Agency approves campus projects, making them eligible for federal funds
1963	*May:* BOT approves contracts for construction of first campus buildings	
1965	*Feb.:* Classes open for two-year program	

CITY OF CHICAGO, COOK COUNTY	HARRISON-HALSTED RESIDENTS, HULL-HOUSE	JOINT ACTION COMMITTEE, OTHER PRIVATE INTERESTED GROUPS
Jan.: City changes site boundaries to exclude area south of Roosevelt Road, to go west instead	*Feb. 8-13:* Discussion in Hull-House BOT of various motions supporting and opposing location decision of city	JAC threatens to appeal state supreme court decision to U.S. Supreme Court
Park District refuses to sell Garfield Park site to University, does not reply to University's request for an answer on this	*Feb. 13:* Motion to take no position on location but to urge public discussion	*Feb. 23:* JAC accepts Harrison-Halsted site
Feb.: Daley meets with University BOT to discuss site	Hull-House BOT interested in its future	Catholic Church accepts city decision
April: Public hearings on site	Area residents meeting in Holy Guardian Angel Church to march on city hall; Scala drafted to head women's group	
May: City Council approves necessary ordinances for campus	Harrison-Halsted Community Group organized, protests at City Hall and all legislative channels	
	Harrison-Halsted group agitates against site decision, protests in all public forums; seeks outside support but is unsuccessful in many of its appeals; appeals to state and federal courts to declare government actions illegal; final appeal rejected by the U.S. Supreme Court in May 1963	

Appendix B

SITE ANALYSIS AND PRELIMINARY PLANS FOR FOUR PROPOSED CAMPUS SITES

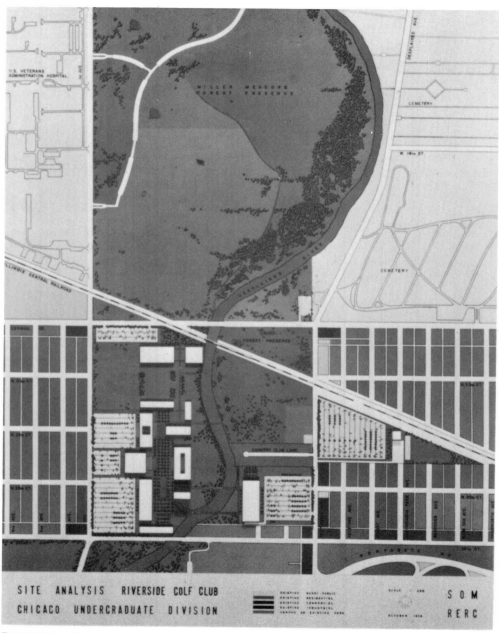

RIVERSIDE GOLF CLUB

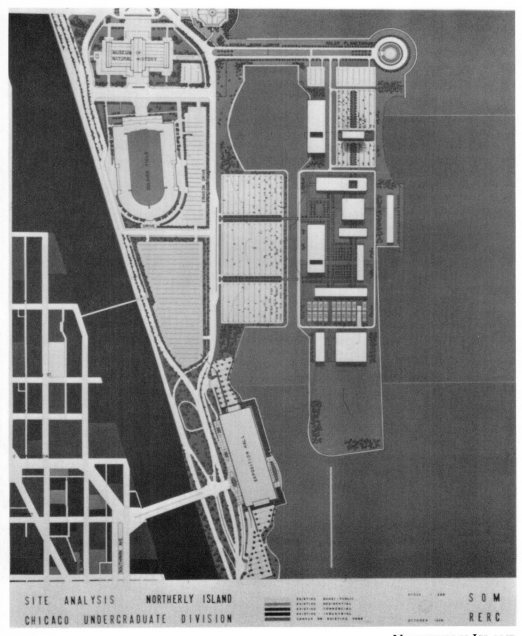

SITE ANALYSIS NORTHERLY ISLAND
CHICAGO UNDERGRADUATE DIVISION

EXISTING QUASI-PUBLIC
EXISTING RESIDENTIAL
EXISTING COMMERCIAL
EXISTING INDUSTRIAL
CAMPUS ON EXISTING LAND

SCALE / 400

OCTOBER 1956

S O M
R E R C

NORTHERLY ISLAND

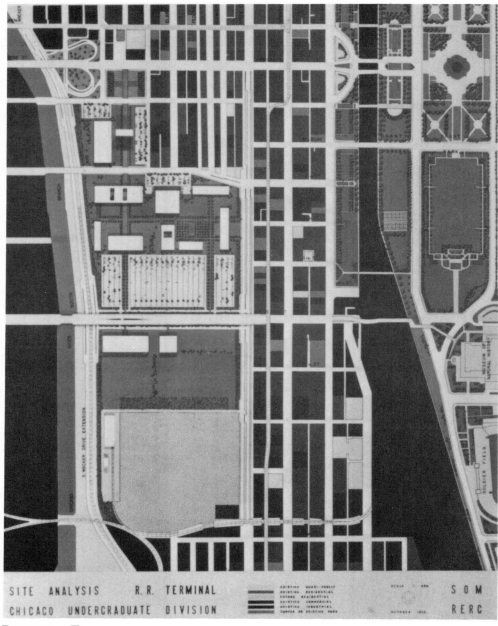

SITE ANALYSIS R.R. TERMINAL
CHICAGO UNDERGRADUATE DIVISION

EXISTING SEMI-PUBLIC
EXISTING RESIDENTIAL
FUTURE RESIDENTIAL
EXISTING COMMERCIAL
EXISTING INDUSTRIAL
CAMPUS OR EXISTING PARK

SCALE 1" 600

OCTOBER 1955

S O M
R E R C

RAILROAD TERMINAL

GARFIELD PARK

Index

Federal government, 165; and site decision, 161–62

Federal Housing and Home Finance Agency, 117

Federal Housing Authority, 142

Field Foundation, 107

Flex-Rite, 141

Flynn, Charles, 25

Forest Preserve District, 17, 18, 35–36, 44, 45, 46, 62, 166

Gage: Farm site, 50, 51; Park site, 53

Galesburg, 20

G. A. Miller Meadows. *See* Miller Meadows

Garden Court, 143

Garfieldian, 76

Garfield Park, 35, 49, 65, 66, 74, 84, 116, 123, 167, 169; and 1958 report, 56; and Board of Trustees, 58, 66, 76; community and location of campus, 67; opposition to 67–68; and planning studies, 72; and Daley, 69; and Henry, 79; problems with, 90

Gately, James, 67

Geyer, Georgie Ann, 115, 118

Giovangelo, Ernest, 107, 108, 109; and Hull-House, 99–100; on Harrison-Halsted protest meeting, 114

Granata, Representative, 117

Great Chicago Fire, 94

Greeks: in Harrison-Halsted area, 96–97; businessmen and Hull-House, 110; and Harrison-Halsted Community Group, 119

Greenfield, Jeff, 15

Griffith, Provost, 31

Haring, Tibor, 109

Harrington, Judge, 77, 80, 91

Harrison-Halsted area: alternative to Terminal site, 73; and city, 77–79; Italians in, 94–96; history of, 94–97; response of, 94–121; Greeks in, 96–97; and politics, 98–99; community planning after World War II, 101–12; 1958 redevelopment plan for, 110–11; relations with campus, 120–21; reasons for choice of, 122; consequences for, 126–56; population changes in, 128–32; housing in and campus, 132–33; and number of

workers and campus, 133–34; campus and land values in, 135–38; amounts invested in, 142–43; housing prices in, 143–47; rents in, 145; and economic impact of campus, 147–49; and family incomes, 149; students from, 149–50; negative effects of campus, 150–55; and technical approach, 166

Harrison-Halsted community, 6; and decision-making, 19; lack of response from, 86–87; and student customs, 155

Harrison-Halsted Community Group, 116, 123, 176; and the courts, 117–18; and "clout," 118–19; and city bond issue, 120

Harrison-Halsted project, 56, 105

Harrison-Halsted residents: and University location, 114–16

Harrison-Halsted Residents' and Businessmen's Association, 110

Harrison-Halsted site, 4, 22; described, 82; Daley's motives, 83–84; and politics, 84–85; and corruption, 85; and Italian political control, 86; problems with, 90; importance of availability of, 92; and deterioration, 139; and displacement of persons and businesses, 141; and city government's support of, 167

Harris Trust, 48

Harvey, David, 8

Havens, Charles S., 5, 25, 76, 78, 111, 116; and Committee on Future Development of Chicago Undergraduate Division, 32; and Chicago campus, 40, 41; and Miller Meadows, 43; and Chicago Central Area Committee, 48; and Gage Farm site, 50; and Bach, 51–52; and Navy Pier, 54; and need for decision, 65, 72; and Harrison-Halsted site, 80, 81–82; memos comparing Harrison-Halsted and Garfield Park, 92

Henry, David Dodds, 5, 6, 21–22, 112, 116; background of, 24; strategy of, 40–41; and Miller Meadows site, 39, 42, 43; and funds, 43; and Terminal site, 49; on importance of Daley, 51; and Peters, 59; address, 1959, 71; and Wayne State, 74; and private colleges, 75–76; and Garfield Park, 77, 79; meeting with Maxwell, 90; promise not to expand, 119